ABBA

—— AT 50 ——

ABBA
— AT 50 —

CARL MAGNUS PALM

PALAZZO

CONTENTS

First published in 2022 by
Palazzo Editions Ltd
15 Church Road
London, SW13 9HE
www.palazzoeditions.com

Text © 2022 Carl Magnus Palm
Design and layout copyright © 2022 Palazzo Editions Ltd
Designed by Becky Clarke for Palazzo Editions

Every effort has been made to trace and acknowledge the copyright holders. If any unintentional omission has occurred, we would be pleased to add an appropriate acknowledgment in any future edition of the book.

A CIP catalogue record for this book is available from the British Library.

ISBN 978-1-78675-101-0

Bound and printed in China

10 9 8 7 6 5 4 3 2 1

COVER ABBA at the BBC, 1974

PAGE 2 ABBA on their folkpark tour of Sweden, 1973, fresh from their success with *Ring Ring*

Introduction

"It's this thing about how reality is stranger than fiction, which is really true. Afterwards, it's hard to see what an insane bloody story the ABBA story is. It did happen, but write our story as a piece of fiction and no-one would find it realistic."

Speaking four decades after ABBA first recorded together, Björn Ulvaeus was on to something crucial. Today, we tend to take Sweden's considerable impact on the popular music scene for granted. In the United States, Max Martin—the Swedish popmeister writer-producer behind mega-hits by everyone from Britney Spears, Katy Perry, and Taylor Swift to Justin Timberlake and The Weeknd—ranks below only John Lennon and Paul McCartney in the number of chart-topping hits. In the twenty-first century, Swedish songwriters and producers are high currency on the international music scene, and although the United States and the United Kingdom remain the strongest forces within popular music, Sweden has now ranked as number three on that list for more than two decades.

But back in 1972, when Agnetha Fältskog, Björn Ulvaeus, Benny Andersson, and Anni-Frid "Frida" Lyngstad first recorded an English-language pop song together, there was very little reason to believe that they had any chance of achieving any major hits abroad, much less a sustained career. As for music written and recorded outside the English-speaking countries, recent years had produced the odd inroad into the important US and UK markets. From the Netherlands, for example, Shocking Blue hit it big with 1969's magnificent "Venus," while Mouth & MacNeal enjoyed a US Top Ten hit in 1972 with the catchy "How Do You Do."

Sweden's space-suit-wearing instrumental guitar band The Spotnicks scored four early 1960s Top Forty hits and a Top Twenty album in the UK, just before The Beatles blew that kind of music out of the water, but enjoyed continued popularity in countries such as France and Japan, their global record sales now estimated at an impressive eighteen million. There were also other Swedish artists who had enjoyed the odd one-off hit in the lower regions of the US charts. Taken altogether, though, there wasn't any massive interest in pop music from Continental Europe, much less from Sweden.

So, what chance for international success for a group initially sporting the impossibly unpractical tongue-twister name of Björn & Benny, Agnetha & Anni-Frid? Why would anyone outside Scandinavia even take the time to listen to their records, however catchy they may be? After all, there was already an abundance of similar chart-friendly music, particularly in countries such as the US and the UK, performed by acts that were conveniently available in those countries and not in some remote nation in the northernmost part of Europe. Yet, as Björn observed, "it did happen," and the ABBA story—and its aftermath—stand as one of the great tales of the popular music era. The group and all the offshoots

LEFT ABBA, 1972. (Back L-R) Björn Ulvaeus, Benny Andersson, (Front L-R) Anni-Frid "Frida" Lyngstad, Agnetha Fältskog

of its legacy, primarily the global juggernaut that is the *Mamma Mia!* musical and movies, have arguably made ABBA's music bigger and more widespread today than it was during the height of their 1970s popularity.

The combination of the four members that made up ABBA was unlikely enough. A naïve, blonde former dance band singer who had scored several big hits in Sweden but who showed no signs of being ready for an international career. A Norwegian-born brunette singer who had grown up in a small Swedish town and spent a decade singing in dance bands, but who, despite several opportunities for a breakthrough, never seemed to win the hearts of a wider audience. And two male former pop stars, enormously successful in the 1960s, but now envisioning a future as a behind-the-scenes writer-producer team. Add to that the two singers striking up romantic relationships with one half each of that writer-producer team, and you're heading straight into that piece of fiction that "no-one would find realistic," as if it were some dime-store romance novel intended for a readership that needed to distract themselves with improbable fairy tales. All that's missing is Judy Garland, Mickey Rooney, and an outburst of "Let's put on the show right here!" Yet, this part of the ABBA story was also one hundred percent real.

Despite what seemed like formidable opposition from an international music industry that wasn't terribly curious about what Swedish writers and performers may have to offer, ABBA managed to find a place in the spotlight. It happened thanks to their victory in the 1974 Eurovision Song Contest with "Waterloo"—and once they had made the breakthrough, they weren't going to let it go without a fight. In these endeavors they owe a lot to their manager, Stig Anderson—that unique combination of perceptive, rational, and ambitious self-made man and short-tempered workaholic—who saw their potential and believed in their chance of becoming globally successful before they themselves did. Already with about twenty years' experience in the music business by the time ABBA broke through, his ingenuity in finding ways to reach out across Sweden's borders, his attitude of regarding

what seemed to be a setback as simply a step on the way, and his conviction that nothing should be left to chance, even if it meant endless plane trips across the planet for personal meetings, were crucial assets in achieving that which many thought was impossible.

Stig was, of course, greatly helped in that the music he was trying to bring to the world was so appealing. While ABBA's earliest recordings were of the light-pop variety, nicely produced and performed, but without offering music critics much to sink their teeth in, a sense of ambition and excitement at exploring the possibilities of the recording studio permeates even their first album, 1973's *Ring Ring*, particularly the title track. In its own way, ABBA's musical development, from their cheerful debut single, "People Need Love," to heartbreak masterpieces such as "The Winner Takes It All" toward the end of their career, is just as astonishing as that of The Beatles going from "Love Me Do" to "Strawberry Fields Forever" within a few years. Naturally, ABBA's not-so-secret weapon was the visual appeal and vocal prowess of their two lead vocalists, Agnetha and Frida. As Agnetha once phrased it, "we sang for all we were worth," and their multilayered harmonies constituted the most crucial part of the famed ABBA sound.

Fate also decreed that ABBA's musical evolution would intertwine with their personal lives, as both

OPPOSITE ABBA pose for the cameras, summer 1977
ABOVE RIGHT ABBA manager Stig "Stikkan" Anderson

marriages within the group broke down and those experiences began to color their musical output. Without having planned it, ABBA offered the world not only pop music of the highest order, but also a psychodrama, onto which the public could project their own experiences, dreams, and fears, as they watched the four members' lives evolve on the world stage. Once ABBA had settled into worldwide popularity, their lyrics, mainly written by Björn, left behind their earlier "we just need some words to sing" philosophy and moved into realistic reflections on the ups and downs in the lives of the everyday man and woman. It's hardly surprising that ABBA appealed to so many people across the globe, young and old: There may have been a bright, inviting sheen to their music, but once they'd lured you in, they confronted you with narratives and vocal performances that could reduce grown men and women to tears.

In the midst of all this, the group experienced insane fandom in Australia that scarred one member for many years to come; managed to conquer country after country despite skeptic naysayers; faced massive criticism at home and abroad for the supposedly crass commercialism of their music; struggled to find a balance between the need for a private life and the requirements of an international career; and got caught up in complex bartering and tax avoidance schemes that ended up losing them millions of kronor.

This Swedish group, with their unique mix of UK- and US-influenced pop and rock, Swedish folk music, Italian ballads, German schlager, and French chansons, was an unlikely prospect for global stardom. Yet it was that very unlikeliness, their willingness to accept whatever influences came their way, not caring whether it was considered cool as

long as it struck an emotional chord within their own souls, that made them so successful.

And now, fifty years since they first began recording together, and in the spirit of reality being stranger than fiction, let's celebrate that "insane story." For Björn was absolutely right: It really did happen.

66 **We sang for all we were worth. 99**

Agnetha

OPPOSITE ABBA live onstage at Wembley Arena, London, 1979

BELOW ABBA filming a television special in Poland, October 1976

BEFORE
ABBA

Before ABBA

S unday, June 5, 1966 was a particularly sunny afternoon on the Ålleberg hill, situated some ten kilometers from the small Swedish town of Falköping. The Hep Stars, Sweden's biggest pop band at the time, had just finished their gig at the top of the hill, which flattens out to a plateau, lending itself to all sorts of festivities. The band, counting the long-haired nineteen-year-old keyboardist Benny Andersson among its members, were out on a so-called *folkpark* tour. Most popular Swedish artists would tour these open-air venues during the summer months; with

shows often lasting no longer than thirty minutes, some acts could squeeze in as many as three shows per day.

The Hep Stars were driving down the narrow gravel road leading from the hill in a fleet of American cars, when another entourage on its way up the hill made it necessary for them to slow down so that they could pass each other. Squeezed together in a rather less glamorous Volvo were the members of The Hootenanny Singers, of which twenty-one-year-old Björn Ulvaeus was a member. This band's repertoire

PAGE 12 One of the earliest publicity shots of the band that was to become ABBA, promoting their forthcoming cabaret show Festfolk, 1970

OPPOSITE Agnetha Fältskog during her early solo career, c.1968

LEFT The Hep Stars (L-R) Benny Andersson, Janne Frisk, Svenne Hedlund, Lennart Hegland, Christer Petterson

<blockquote>
❝ It actually wasn't very good, but at least it was an attempt—a first attempt at working together. ❞

Benny
</blockquote>

BELOW Björn Ulvaeus with his parents Gunnar and Aina Ulvaeus in 1971

OPPOSITE Where it all began. Benny Andersson (L) and Björn Ulvaeus (R), just hours before they wrote their first song, June 1966.

was mainly Swedish folk/light-pop songs, and their hair wasn't quite as long as that of The Hep Stars, who at the time dealt exclusively in English pop and rock 'n' roll. The Hootenanny Singers were now on their way up to a thirty-minute gig on the hill, the group being almost as big a live draw as The Hep Stars.

As they slowed down, the two bands couldn't help noticing that they had happened upon a competing group. Windows were wound down and they said hello. That evening, The Hootenanny Singers were planning a farewell party for three of the band's four members, who were due to start their mandatory military service the following day. They invited The Hep Stars to come to the hotel in the town of Linköping, where they were going to have the party. The Hep Stars, never missing the chance of a bit of nighttime fun, readily agreed.

Late that night they arrived at the party, by that time in full swing. The group of rowdy youngsters were soon asked to leave the hotel, ending up in a nearby park, playing acoustic guitars and singing Beatles songs. In that warm summer dawn, there was an instant connection between Björn and Benny. At the time, The Hep Stars were at No. 1 with their latest hit single, "Wedding," a co-write between Benny and Hep

Stars lead singer Svenne Hedlund. An excited Björn told Benny how "bloody catchy" he thought "Wedding" was. At the same time, The Hootenanny Singers were in the charts with a song written by Björn, the folk-poppy "No Time," one of his attempts to drag the band into English-language pop territory, so Benny would have been aware that he was talking to someone who also had ambitions in the songwriting department. In their tipsy state they agreed that it would be fun to write a song together sometime, probably not knowing whether it would ever happen.

But just a couple of weeks later the two bands met up at another party, this time in a cabin outside The Hootenanny Singers' hometown of Västervik, on Sweden's east coast. In the middle of the night, Björn and Benny decided that they would try to write that song. They drove to the apartment building where Björn's family lived and began setting up their equipment—an electric organ, amplifiers—in the basement. The noise was enough to rouse Björn's dad, Gunnar, who came rushing down and told them that they had to stop immediately. "You're going to wake up the entire building!" he told them. Gunnar may have been upset, but he still came up with a solution

for the two young men who were so excited about the prospect of writing a song together. Daddy Ulvaeus was employed at the local paper mill and gave Björn the keys to their office: No one was there in the middle of the night and they could play away to their hearts' content without disturbing anyone.

Off they went, enlisting the help of roadies to drag their equipment up the narrow stairs to the office. "I remember very well how Benny and I found our way up the stairs; at first we couldn't find the light switch, so we had to make our way through the darkness," Björn related. All the equipment set up, they began writing what would become the first Andersson/Ulvaeus composition. "Isn't It Easy to Say" is a pleasant if rather hesitant pop-waltz, recorded by The Hep Stars later that year; listening to it, you can almost sense how the two songwriters are trying to find a way to work together. Benny would later admit that it "actually wasn't very good, but at least it was an attempt—a first attempt at working together."

The writing of this fairly unremarkable song, at a paper mill in a small Swedish town, marks the start of the ABBA story.

If the four members of ABBA had anything in common beyond their talent for creating glorious pop music, it was the fact that they all started singing and playing when they were quite young. Also, they were still in their teens when they turned professional. This explains why they were all able to conduct fairly long pre-ABBA careers of varying degrees of success, yet still be relatively young when ABBA had their breakthrough in the 1970s.

BJÖRN ULVAEUS, the oldest member, was born on April 25, 1945 in Gothenburg on Sweden's west coast. The family moved to the town of Västervik when Björn was about six years old, as his father, Gunnar, gained employment at his brother's paper mill. Björn's mother, Aina, was a housewife for most of his youth; in 1948, the family welcomed a daughter, Eva. Björn would later have mixed feelings about his childhood: On the one hand, he grew up in a safe and rather idyllic small town, going home from school on lunch breaks to be served a meal by his mother, but on the other, his parents did not have a happy marriage and his father was maybe a little too fond of drinking. Later in life he would admit to himself that Gunnar had actually let him down on several occasions in his youth, which had instilled a sense of worry and insecurity in Björn that would dog him through the years.

Music was a comfort and something to hold on to, though, entering his life for real in 1957, when he was twelve years old. His cousin Joen was very musical and had started Joen's Skiffle Group, skiffle being a fairly basic variant of American folk music, with influences from blues and jazz. The genre became popular in the mid-1950s in the UK through artists such as Lonnie Donegan, with washboards and tea-chest basses often making up the rhythm section. Björn was excited by the prospect of playing with the band and begged his parents to buy him a guitar. This they did and he joined his cousin's band. From that moment on, music was the main focus of Björn's life.

The band eventually morphed into a Dixieland band, but by the early 1960s they were ready to break up.

LEFT Björn Ulvaeus with The Hootenanny Singers performing on a TV show in 1966, in Hamburg, Germany

OPPOSITE Stig Anderson with some of the artists he represented. (L-R) Björn Ulvaeus, Benny Andersson, Hansi Schwarz, Ted Gärdestad, Tonny Roth, and Agnetha Fältskog (left) and Frida Lyngstad (right) flanking Stig (center) in the front row

The bass player in the band was Björn's friend Tonny Roth, who now got an offer to join a folk group calling themselves The Partners. This band was led by an aficionado of American folk music, Hansi Schwarz, who was especially enamored with the music and repertoire of The Kingston Trio, of "Tom Dooley" fame. Tonny said that he would only join The Partners if his pal Björn could come along as well. But, as Björn would recall, "I don't think Hansi was too happy about that, because they already had three guitar players and it wasn't like they really needed a fourth one." Nevertheless, Hansi had to accept Tonny's conditions, so Björn was in.

Eventually, they learned that there was another Swedish band called The Partners, so they changed their name to The West Bay Singers, "West Bay" being a direct translation of Västervik. Björn soon emerged as the major talent in the group in terms of arranging their vocal harmonies, removing whatever doubts Hansi may have had about him. By 1963, the band, all the members of which were still in high school, had

lost one of their guitarists and were down to a more manageable quartet. In September of that year they decided to enter a talent contest arranged by Sveriges Radio, the equivalent of the UK's BBC.

Even at the preliminary heats, a major Swedish newspaper, reporting from the contest, singled out the group as particularly talented. This article piqued the interest of two men who had just formed the record company Polar Music in Stockholm. Bengt Bernhag and Stig Anderson had both been active in the music industry for about a decade—Bernhag as a record producer, Anderson primarily as a songwriter and music publisher—and they were now looking for talent to sign to their brand-new label. The West Bay Singers were contacted and asked to send a demo tape to Polar, which they promptly did. The reaction was very favorable indeed: Stig Anderson took it upon himself to travel to Västervik to secure the services of this promising band.

Stig was born on January 25, 1931 and, like the ABBA members, had an early start in music, writing

his first hit at age sixteen, even though it would take a few years before it was issued on disc. The 1950s had seen him trying a bit of everything within the entertainment industry—performing in *folkparks*, writing songs that were recorded either by himself or other artists—and working as a teacher in a Stockholm suburb to make ends meet. Some of his songs became hits, while others bombed, but in 1960 he enjoyed his biggest success so far with a song called "Är du kär i mig ännu, Klas-Göran" ("Are You Still In Love with Me, Klas-Göran"), performed by the immensely popular singer Lill-Babs. The financial windfall of this No. 1 smash prompted him to start his own publishing company and leave his job as a teacher.

After a very lean couple of years—on some days, Stig and his family wondered if they could even afford to buy food—he began enjoying huge success in acquiring the publishing rights to foreign hits and then writing Swedish lyrics for them. His first major hit in this field was "Sånt är livet" ("That's Life"), a version of Roy Hamilton's "You Can Have Her." As recorded by singer Anita Lindblom, it spent five weeks at No. 1 in 1962. In the course of the decade, Stig would become by far the most prolific lyricist in Sweden, churning out lyrics in the nighttime and taking care of business in

the daytime, traveling all over the planet, and working more or less 365 days a year. Meanwhile, Bengt Bernhag had the main responsibility for Polar Music and its artists.

Back in 1963, Stig managed to persuade The West Bay Singers that Polar Music was the right record company for them. However, he and Bengt felt that they needed to change their name. In the world of early 1960s American folk music, a hootenanny was an event inviting participation from the audience, where singers known and unknown were encouraged to perform. Much to the dismay of the group, Stig and Bengt now decided that their new discovery was going to be called The Hootenanny Singers. "It's the worst name that any group has ever had," said Björn many years later.

Before long, the group, new name and all, was in a Stockholm studio, recording their first single and EP for Polar Music. "Jag väntar vid min mila" ("I'm Waiting at the Stack") was a Swedish folk-style song performed in a Kingston Trio arrangement and it became an instant hit. Immediately after the group graduated from high school in June 1964, when Björn was still only nineteen, they embarked on a successful *folkpark* tour and over the next couple of years notched up a string of hits.

BENNY ANDERSSON is the only true Stockholmer in ABBA, born in Sweden's capital on December 16, 1946. His father was a construction engineer named Gösta, while his mother Laila was a housewife; Benny also had a younger sister, Eva-Lis, born in 1948. For the first few years of Benny's life, the family moved around a bit, before settling in the newly built suburb of Vällingby, west of Stockholm, in 1955. Although he worked in construction, Gösta loved playing the accordion, as did Benny's grandfather Efraim.

It was almost inevitable that Benny would get an accordion on his sixth birthday, and he began playing together with his father and grandfather. It was mainly his grandfather who would teach him, though. "Everyone should have someone who has the patience to play together with you even though you really can't play, and without telling you that you can't play. My grandfather was like that," Benny recalled. Together, the three generations of Andersson men would occasionally perform at dances and such, calling themselves Benny's Trio in an affectionate nod to their youngest member.

Grandfather Efraim would also be instrumental in securing a piano for Benny. In 1957, when Efraim

and his wife sold their house and moved to an apartment, their grandchildren were given some money. Benny's parents decided that the funds should be used to buy their ten-year-old son a piano. From that moment on, Benny claims, not a single day has gone by when he hasn't played the piano: He became one of those rare people for whom music is an ingrained part of their entire being. If he happens to spot a keyboard, wherever he may be, he can't resist playing it.

As a teenager, Benny played with a number of local bands, one of which featured his girlfriend Christina on vocals. In Benny's relationship with Christina, one thing led to another, and he was still only sixteen when their son, Peter, was born in August 1963. Two years later, they had a daughter named Heléne. Both parents being so young, it was never a family in the traditional sense. By 1966, the relationship was over, and the children were mainly being raised by their mother.

In the autumn of 1964, an up-and-coming Stockholm rock 'n' roll band called The Hep Stars lost their organist. Impressed with Benny's keyboard skills, they asked him if he wanted to join them. The seventeen-

OPPOSITE
The Hep Stars in Stockholm's Gustaf Vasa church at a photo session for a Christmas single, 1967

RIGHT Benny, 1969

year old student said yes on the spot, dropping out of high school in the process.

In the spring of 1965, The Hep Stars got the chance to appear on Swedish TV's main pop music program, *Drop In*. Performing their latest single, "Cadillac"—a reworked version of Vince Taylor's early British rock classic "Brand New Cadillac"—and offering a wild stage show, The Hep Stars made an indelible impression on the young audience glued to their television sets. Before long, the band had three singles in the charts at the same time, marking the start of a career that would make them Sweden's biggest pop band in record time, constantly touring and dashing off several hundred gigs per year.

Initially, The Hep Stars had been reliant on cover versions of songs by artists such as The Kinks, The Rolling Stones, and Elvis Presley. But Lennon and McCartney's success with their songs for The Beatles created a climate in which bands should preferably write their own material. Many of The Hep Stars' competing bands did indeed write their own songs and it was becoming a bit of an embarrassment. "None of the five members is a composer talent and therefore they don't have any songs of their own in their show—homemade melodies is otherwise a staple of most pop bands these days," noted one newspaper. The

situation changed in the summer of 1965, when Benny decided to have a go. The result was a song called "No Response," which, excepting a few long-forgotten instrumentals, was Benny's first composition. Released as a single in the autumn of 1965, "No Response" shot to No. 2—it wasn't a particularly great piece of music, so one suspects that much of its success was thanks to the enormous popularity of The Hep Stars. Nevertheless, Benny's confidence must have been boosted. He could now call himself a songwriter.

In February 1966, he sat down at the piano again, while The Hep Stars were on tour in Norway. This time the outcome was all the more impressive: The tender, spinet-driven ballad "Sunny Girl" showed a real talent for melody. When released as a single by The Hep Stars that spring, it spent five consecutive weeks at No. 1 on the sales chart. At the time, Sweden also had a vote-based radio chart, presented in a program called *Tio i topp* ("The Top Ten"). This chart, attracting millions of listeners to its Saturday afternoon broadcasts, was actually more important than the sales chart, as success on it could help artists secure lucrative *folkpark* gigs and television appearances.

When the exciting news that "Sunny Girl" had reached No. 1 on *Tio i topp* reached him, nineteen-year-old Benny was with The Hep Stars at a venue

in the town of Kungsbacka, preparing for a gig. "Everybody was damned happy, of course, but I was really happy," he recalled. "I remember that I went into the dressing room to be alone for a while. I might even have shed a tear or two. Because then I knew that I had done a good song, and I could also relate to why it was good, that it grabbed hold of my feelings. Then I thought, 'If I can do a song like that, I should be able to make two—and if I can do two, I can probably make three,' and so on. There, in Kungsbacka, I decided for the first time what I was going to do with my life, and I was pretty shaken by that feeling. I thought, 'Now I don't have to wonder whether I'll be a taxi driver or a construction engineer, or whatever I'm going to do after The Hep Stars; this is what I'm going to do from now on.'"

> **❝ I knew that I had done a good song, and I could also relate to why it was good, that it grabbed hold of my feelings. ❞**
>
> Benny

OPPOSITE Benny with The Hep Stars (center, on keyboard)
BELOW Back row: Björn (L) and Benny (R) with former lead singers of The Hep Stars, front row: Svenne (L) and Lotta Hedlund (R). The quartet toured a cabaret show 1969–1970.

ABOVE Benny and Frida who met in 1969

They had neglected to pay taxes on their vast earnings and were now stuck with a tax bill that would dog the members well into the 1970s. Benny remembered that it took him four years of being put "on pocket money" to be completely free of his tax debt.

Adding to the financial problems, those seemingly inevitable "musical differences" were also causing friction within the group. By 1969, the group were enjoying success in cabaret, dressed up in uniform stage costumes, and were having hits with light-pop material in Swedish. It was a far cry from the rock 'n' roll of their early career, and some of the members didn't like the development. Benny, Svenne, and his wife, Charlotte Walker—an American singer who joined The Hep Stars in 1968—argued that they should go on with the cabaret, while the other members felt differently. A split was inevitable: Benny, Svenne, and Charlotte left after they had concluded the band's 1969 summer tour, while the other members continued as The Hep Stars.

Björn was having parallel experiences in The Hootenanny Singers. In 1969, the group lost one of its members and was down to a trio, but after their summer tour of that year they were a band that almost only existed in the recording studio. The other members were conducting university studies, while Björn, who had moved to Stockholm and begun studying, dropped out when the pull of the music business turned out to be stronger than any prospects of an ordinary job. Parallel with his group recordings, he had also begun a solo career, issuing a number of singles.

By this time, Björn and Benny had become best friends and decided to intensify their collaboration, starting a partnership as songwriters and producers. Crucially, after enjoying an existence as teen idols for several years, they were now looking forward to a career behind the scenes. For the time being they would tour together and release records as a duo, but the goal was to gradually ease out of being performers themselves.

Another important aspect of both their lives had changed in the spring of 1969. It began in March of that year, when Benny entered into his first long-term romantic relationship.

His co-write with Svenne Hedlund, "Wedding," was the follow-up to "Sunny Girl" and also reached No. 1 on the charts, making an impression on Björn Ulvaeus. Björn himself had tried to get the songwriting going since 1965, having had his first songs, "Time to Move Along" and "No Time," included on The Hootenanny Singers' fourth album, *International*, issued toward the end of 1965. When he and Benny met up for the first time, they recognized that they both played the same role in their respective groups: They were pretty much the only ones who were interested in songwriting, and that forged an immediate and strong bond between them.

Not many Andersson/Ulvaeus songs emerged over the next few years, though, as they were busy with their groups, both of which continued to have hits and tour successfully across Sweden. The year 1967 was probably the peak for The Hep Stars, who expanded their audience when they began recording in Swedish, parallel with their English-language songs: On their summer *folkpark* tour that year, they performed more than two hundred gigs in four months. But just a few months later, in December, The Hep Stars' irresponsible attitude to finances came crashing down on them.

ANNI-FRID LYNGSTAD had a background that was far more dramatic than that of any of her three colleagues in ABBA. Born on November 15, 1945 in the small town of Ballangen in northern Norway, she was the product of a liaison between Alfred Haase, a German soldier in the occupying forces during World War II, and Synni Lyngstad, a Norwegian teenager. Alfred left Norway long before Anni-Frid was born and for many years the Lyngstad family thought he had perished on his way back to Germany. Because of the difficult situation for women who had committed the unforgivable crime of fraternizing with German soldiers, Synni and her mother, Anni, took Anni-Frid with them and moved to Sweden in 1947. Making a new life for themselves wasn't going to be easy, but at least they had a fresh start. However, no sooner had they settled in Sweden than tragedy struck. In September 1947, Synni collapsed and was taken to hospital with a kidney disease. This was about fifteen years before dialysis came into wide use in Sweden, and on September 28, Synni, who was still only twenty-one, died. Her daughter, Anni-Frid, was not yet two years old.

ABOVE Anni-Frid Lyngstad, 1967

Anni-Frid would be brought up by her grandmother, Anni—herself a widow—in a small town called Torshälla, some 90 kilometers west of Stockholm. Despite a financially strained situation, Anni made sure that her granddaughter had all the basic material comforts. But the age difference and Anni's somewhat austere personality meant that there was never a strong emotional bond between them, Anni-Frid craving a kind of love that her grandmother was unable to give her.

Fortunately, music was there as an escape. As Anni-Frid would phrase it later in life, she didn't start singing—she always sang. In school, she was an ambitious and well-behaved pupil, but as early as age seven, Anni-Frid knew that she wanted to become a singer. "I never even considered doing anything else," she would remember. For a while she took piano lessons, but singing was her main interest.

She was only thirteen years old when she was at a local dance and plucked up the courage to ask the band if they would let her sing a few songs with them. The band said yes and before long she had been asked to join them as their permanent vocalist. Around this time she acquired the nickname Frida, which most of her friends and family, and eventually her audience, would call her. For most of the following decade, she would be a vocalist in a number of local dance bands. Frida had an ambitious personality, was dedicated to music, and determined that the bands she was in should rehearse as often as possible.

In one of the bands she met a young man called Ragnar Fredriksson, who soon became her boyfriend. Just like Benny, Frida became a teenage parent when her son, Hans, was born in January 1963. Frida and Ragnar married in April 1964, when the bride was still only eighteen years old. Eventually, they moved to the nearby town of Eskilstuna, and in 1967 a daughter named Ann Lise-Lotte was born.

On the surface it seemed like an idyllic existence in prosperous Sweden, but Frida was struggling to balance her life as a housewife and mother with her ambitions as a singer. Over the years she had entered a number of talent contests, but without her occasional

victories ever leading anywhere. Frida began feeling restless and was wondering if her fate in life was really to remain in Eskilstuna as a housewife and dance band singer. Although not the most confident of women, deep inside she felt she had the talent and ability to make something more of her life.

In 1967, she entered yet another talent contest. This time she went all the way to the finals in Stockholm on September 3. She wooed the audience with a gentle bossa nova entitled "En ledig dag" ("A Day Off") and impressed the jury to the extent that she won the entire contest. But it didn't end there. After accepting her prize, Frida thought she was going to drive back to her home in Eskilstuna, not knowing that there was a secret agreement with the producers of a major talk show that the winner of the contest would appear on live television that evening. So, Frida was

whisked away in a car to the television studios and asked to perform her winning song, with the studio band having only minutes to study the sheet music and whip up an arrangement for the song. Everything went off without a hitch, though, and twenty-one-year-old Frida impressed the millions of viewers. "It's like a dream," the rather shaken young singer told a reporter afterwards.

The Swedish music business also pricked up its ears. Only a week later she had been signed to a record contract and was in the studio to make a single of the song she had performed on television. Alas, it did not become a hit, and over the next few years, although she released single after single, she had very little success as a recording artist. Despite being in full control of her voice and hitting the notes perfectly, there was something lacking in her performance, a

certain restraint that stopped the general public from truly falling in love with her.

At the same time, Frida's marriage to Ragnar was falling apart as she was itching to break free from her responsibilities and make a go of her singing career. In early 1969, the pair divorced, with the children staying with their dad in Eskilstuna while Frida moved closer to Stockholm to pursue her dreams of stardom. She began working in cabaret with popular pianist Charlie Norman and his show, remaining with him for the better part of eighteen months.

In March 1969, when the Norman show was in southern Sweden, she happened to run into Benny and Björn at a restaurant; they were also in town performing in cabaret with The Hep Stars (Björn was a temporary replacement for the band's regular guitarist). There was an immediate spark between

ABOVE Frida performs with musician Charlie Norman, 1969
OPPOSITE Frida Lyngstad pictured together with her first husband Ragnar and children Hans and Lise-Lotte in Eskilstuna, 1967

the cute young keyboardist and the brunette with the infectious laugh. When they met on a radio show again later the same month, they went to dinner afterwards and before long Benny and Frida were an item and had moved in together. In August, they were engaged.

By that time, Björn had also entered into his first serious relationship.

The town of Jönköping is situated in the province of Småland, the same area of Sweden where Björn's hometown of Västervik is located. **AGNETHA FÄLTSKOG** was born in Jönköping on April 5, 1950 and this is also where she would grow up. Her father, Ingvar, was a store manager, while her mother, Birgit, was a housewife. In 1955, Agnetha's sister, Mona, was born.

It was, by all accounts, a pretty secure and idyllic childhood. "My mother was always at home, and we had firm routines and regular schedules that we lived by," Agnetha recalled. "When I got home from school my mother was there, and at ten past five every day daddy came home from work. And then you went to bed at a certain time and got up at a certain time."

Ingvar had a keen interest in performing and would stage amateur revues in Jönköping, writing skits and songs for the shows. It didn't amount to anything more than a certain local notoriety, but he enjoyed doing it. No doubt, some of that interest in singing and writing songs rubbed off on his oldest daughter, who began playing the piano at age five, writing her first song, "Två små troll" ("Two Little Trolls"), a year later. Around the same time, Agnetha made her stage debut as a singer at a local party, arranged by her father. It seems the most memorable part of her performance was when the elastic of her panties snapped, causing them to slide slowly down beneath her dress while she was singing. As Agnetha's parents remembered, the audience was roaring with laughter.

By her early teens, Agnetha was a productive songwriter, getting together with a couple of friends to form a girl trio and performing in local revues and such. Graduating from junior secondary school at age fifteen, she found work as a switchboard operator at a local car firm, all the while writing songs and singing on and off with different bands in the Jönköping area.

She was sixteen when she was asked to join Bernt Enghardt's dance band, doing her first show with them as a permanent member on September 17, 1966. The band, which was a rather big name locally, featured a horn section and tried to incorporate as many soul numbers as possible in their repertoire. As improbable as it may seem, Agnetha actually sang the lead on James Brown's classic soul shouter "I Got You (I Feel Good)." She loved singing with the band, but her mother worried that it would be too much to work all week at the switchboard and then sing with the band on the weekends. After all, she said, shouldn't a teenage girl relax sometimes, see friends, and have fun? For Agnetha the choice was easy: She wanted to sing.

TOP Birgit and Ingvar Fältskog, parents of Agnetha
ABOVE Agnetha (born Åse Agneta Fältskog) age 13 in a school photograph from 1963
OPPOSITE Agnetha during her early solo career

> ❝ **It was the happiest moment of my whole career in music** ❞
>
> Agnetha

After a few months with Enghardt's, Agnetha plucked up the courage to bring a song of her own to the band. Triggered by the recent breakup with a boyfriend, and inspired by the most maudlin parts of the repertoire of her idol, American singer Connie Francis, she had written a ballad entitled "Jag var så kär" ("I Was So In Love"). The band liked the song immediately and worked out an arrangement for it. It was also included on a demo tape that they sent to Cupol, a record company in Stockholm. The tape piqued the interest of the label—but they were only interested in Agnetha. Before long, she had a record contract as a solo performer.

In October 1967, accompanied by her father, a nervous Agnetha, still only seventeen years old, entered a Stockholm studio to record her first single. One of the sides of the single was that self-written tune, "Jag var så kär." Walking down the steps to the studio, she was overwhelmed by the sound of her own song, orchestrated by a professional arranger and played by a full band, strings and all. "It was the happiest moment of my whole career in music," she remembered.

What happened next went beyond Agnetha's wildest dreams: In February 1968, the song was at No. 1 on the sales chart and immediately established her as a star. Not only was it a sensation that she had success with her very first single, but it was a song she had written herself. In the 1960s, with the exception of artists like American singer Jackie DeShannon and a

LEFT Agnetha, Stockholm, Sweden, 1972

handful of other performers, it was highly unusual that female singers wrote their own material, much less seventeen-year-old girls far removed from the world's showbusiness hotspots.

Agnetha's star may have been in the ascendancy, but she still continued singing with the band and working full-time at the switchboard. Before long, though, the lack of rest and the constant working caught up with her. "One of the girls at work told me that I looked pale—that's the last thing I remember. Then I fainted." Her mother gave her an ultimatum: She had to choose between the switchboard or the singing. Again, Agnetha placed her bet on music, and a few weeks later she was gone from the car firm. She had committed to tour the *folkparks* with Bernt Enghardt's band in the summer of 1968, but at the end of the tour Agnetha left the band and moved to Stockholm to pursue her career as a solo singer. She was doing rather well, notching up hits, taking acting lessons, and even kicking off a recording career in West Germany.

In May 1969, Agnetha was booked to film a Swedish television special on the west coast of Sweden. Among the other artists taking part in the special was a well-known singer called Björn Ulvaeus. She had met him briefly the previous summer, when The Hootenanny Singers and Bernt Enghardt's band performed in the same *folkpark*, but, as Björn later admitted, he had actually fallen in love with her the moment he'd seen her on television for the first time. During the filming of the television special, a romance began between Björn and Agnetha. They moved in together, and in the spring of 1970 they were engaged.

Two couples consisting of four individuals engaged in the music business as songwriters, producers, and performers—by 1970, the scene was clearly set for forming a groovy pop group. But as we shall see, the road to becoming ABBA was anything but straight.

RIGHT
Agnetha and
Björn in 1970

2

THE HAPPIEST
SOUND OF
THEM ALL

The Happiest Sound Of Them All

"The show passes you by without leaving much of a trace."

"Next to the backing band, the performances of the two couples pale significantly."

"If this show had gone on for a further fifteen minutes, I would have needed a teething ring to prevent me from crying out loud."

Not every review of the show *Festfolk*, which opened in Gothenburg on November 1, 1970, was as bad as the extracts presented here—some were even outright positive—but, ironically, these quotes come closest to reflecting the feelings of the stars of the show. For Björn, Benny, Agnetha, and Frida would come to look back on this cabaret concoction as, in Björn's words, "the absolute low point of the careers of everyone involved." But how did they end up at this nadir?

In the course of 1969, Björn and Benny had solidified their collaboration as songwriters, forming a publishing company with Polar Music head honchos Bengt Bernhag and Stig Anderson. The pair had also collaborated as record producers for the first time. Björn was living with Agnetha, and Benny with Frida. Benny was also taking over as producer for Frida, his

first production for her being the October 1969 single "Peter Pan," written by him and Björn: This was the first time that three future ABBA members contributed to the same song. Then, in February 1970, Agnetha sang backing vocals on "There's a Little Man," a song written and produced by Björn and Benny for a singer named Billy G-son, marking her first professional collaboration with the male half of ABBA. Although none of these singles became hits, one could be forgiven for thinking that the stage was set for the formation of a quartet, but it would take a while before that idea took root.

Like so many other Swedish pop stars around this time, Björn and Benny were searching for new identities and roles within the music business. Many of their peers were moving into more progressive rock music or were trying to establish themselves as singer-songwriters, sometimes with overtly political lyrics. This was not Björn and Benny's cup of tea, as they held firm to the idea that music was, first and foremost, entertainment, and as much as they were fans of contemporary pop and rock, they also appreciated a pretty tune and didn't necessarily rate one above the other.

They were also determined to make a living as songwriters and performers, and seemingly jumped on anything that could help them stay afloat. The autumn of 1969 saw them working as a quartet in cabaret together with Svenne and Charlotte Hedlund (known by her Swedish nickname, Lotta), the former lead singers of The Hep Stars. At the same time they were writing songs for various performers, but except for a couple of hits earlier in 1969, they didn't have much success. They even resorted to writing the soundtrack music for a couple of so-called sexploitation films, sexploitation being a retrospective label attached to low-budget films where the plot, such as it was, mainly served to show the actors in various stages of nudity.

As for Agnetha and Frida, they were both active

PAGE 32 ABBA around the time of their performance in the Swedish selection for Eurovision, 1973
OPPOSITE ABBA onstage at the Liseberg amusement park in Gothenburg, Sweden, 1973

The Happiest Sound Of Them All 35

ABOVE Agnetha on tour with actor and singer Bert-Åke Varg (L), in 1970
OPPOSITE (L-R) Agnetha, Björn and Benny, 1971, touring the folkparks without Frida

in their solo careers and, unlike Björn and Benny, not recording for Polar Music but being tied to other labels. Agnetha was having hits every now and then and performing successfully on *folkpark* tours, while the generally hitless Frida was mainly kept occupied through her cabaret collaboration with Charlie Norman. Similar to Björn and Benny, their music was mainly in the field of light-pop and you weren't going to see the two of them on the barricades singing protest songs any time soon. So, there may have been two romantically involved couples, but they kept their careers pretty much separate.

Things changed in April 1970. On Agnetha's twentieth birthday, the two couples traveled to Cyprus, where they had been engaged to perform a little in exchange for a reduced price on their plane tickets. In conjunction with the trip, Agnetha and Björn were engaged; alas, much to Agnetha's fury Björn managed to lose his engagement ring while swimming in the

Mediterranean, as the ring was just slightly too large for his finger.

More important for their future were the performances they did for UN soldiers stationed on the war-ravaged island. The four of them had previously sung together, privately and just for the fun of it, and noticed that it sounded quite good when their voices were combined. Now, singing to a real live audience, they were even more convinced that this was something they should pursue.

For the summer of 1970, all four had *folkpark* tours already sewn up: Björn and Benny were touring with

Svenne and Lotta; Frida had an engagement with Charlie Norman; and Agnetha was touring with a Swedish comedian. All of these tours had a hint of cabaret about them: There were sung numbers, of course, but some of those songs had supposedly funny lyrics and there were also outright skits and such. If you were working within the light entertainment field at that time, this was the kind of show you put on.

Now, for the autumn, Björn, Benny, Agnetha, and Frida, encouraged by their experience in Cyprus, decided to give it a go with a cabaret show as a quartet. Although the two relationships weren't exactly free of friction, the four of them were optimistic about working together, Benny and Frida declaring that they simply had to be together. "If you work separately as artists the relationship ends sooner or later. You experience too much on your own and grow apart."

Together with a couple of lyricists du jour, they devised a show that was entitled *Festfolk*: The title was a pun, as it could mean both "party people" and "engaged couples," depending on the spelling. But when the show opened in Gothenburg on November 1, 1970, it was soon clear that there had been little justification for the couples' optimism about the venture. Trying to be funny onstage didn't come naturally to them, and even the positive reviews lacked genuine enthusiasm. The

general public seemed to read between the lines and decided to stay away. The four would be haunted by memories of only a handful of "yawning car-salesmen" in the audience during some shows.

After a stint in Stockholm in December, the quartet took their show on a short tour in February, which was even more disastrous. Crammed together in a car, driving from one venue to the next on slippery winter roads, they found it hard to get along. However much they may like each other as individuals, the friendships and relationships were still fairly new and they hadn't quite got used to each other's quirks. After the tour, Benny and Frida, who only a few months earlier proclaimed so confidently that they "had to be together," changed their tune. "It's not a good idea to both work and live together," Frida said. "It's easier to get in a bad mood. We sat in the car together, dined together, performed together, checked into the hotel together. It was just too much."

The strain almost put an end to Benny and Frida's relationship. A planned *folkpark* tour for the quartet in the summer of 1971 was reduced to just Björn, Benny, and Agnetha, while Frida went on tour with another singer. As Benny said with some understatement, this was "a happy solution." As for the *Festfolk* experience as a whole, Björn summed it up as a venture where they "learned exactly what we should *not* be doing."

Parallel with this unfortunate experience there were positive signs on the horizon. Since the spring of 1970, Ulvaeus and Andersson had been recording as the duo

Björn & Benny, releasing their first and only long-player around the time of the *Festfolk* opening. The album featured a song entitled "Hej gamle man!" ("Hey Old Man!"), which, with its acoustic guitars, tambourine, and sing-along-friendly chorus, had a bit of a Salvation Army feel to it: The lyrics were actually about a Sally Army soldier. This prompted the duo to invite their fiancées to sing backing vocals on the recording, to get a mix of male and female vocals on it, marking the first time that all four appeared on the same record.

"Hej gamle man!" was released as a single and went to No. 1 on the vote-based radio chart *Svensktoppen* ("The Swedish Top Ten"; this was similar in importance to the *Tio i topp* chart that was so crucial for groups such as The Hep Stars, but the songs on *Svensktoppen* were of the light-pop variety and were sung in Swedish). The single also reached No. 5 on the sales chart. The message was clear: Mediocre cabaret tours aside, there was still plenty of potential in the four singing together. "I don't think ["Hej gamle man!"] would have become such a hit if Agnetha and I hadn't been on it," Frida reflected a couple of decades later.

For a year or so following the less than happy *Festfolk* tour, the four friends mainly kept up their collaboration in the recording studio. Benny kept on producing Frida, while Björn took on Agnetha's recordings, and all four of them would turn up on each of the recordings made by the four, as instrumentalists or backing vocalists. In the autumn of 1971, Frida finally achieved a proper hit in her own name with a Swedish version of a song Benny had originally written for The Hep Stars; unsurprisingly, Benny produced it and played on it, and Agnetha and Björn helped out with backing vocals.

Björn and Agnetha were married in July 1971, during a break in the *folkpark* tour they were conducting with Benny, attracting extensive press coverage and a mass of curious onlookers. In early 1972, the two couples moved to terraced houses in a suburb called Vallentuna, north of Stockholm; if they wanted to hang out, it was only a matter of a short walk of a minute or two. These living arrangements cemented the public's view of them as four basically nice, family-friendly and non-threatening performers within the light-pop genre. The weeklies and the Sunday supplements couldn't get enough of reporting on their cosy domesticity. It was a far cry from anything even resembling the lives of subversive rock stars.

OPPOSITE Frida, 1971
RIGHT Agnetha and Björn get married, July 1971

> **66 If you work separately as artists the relationship ends sooner or later. 99**
> Benny and Frida

The first few years of the 1970s saw many parallel developments, and it's hard to keep track of what happened first, what immediate effect it had, and what, in the long term, it meant for the four members that were to make up ABBA. Perhaps most importantly, in the summer of 1971, Björn and Benny were hired by Stig Anderson as Polar Music house producers. This was the consequence of a tragic event taking place on the day of Björn and Agnetha's wedding. Bengt Bernhag, Stig's forty-three-year-old partner in Polar, had been suffering from colitis for almost a decade, causing him to grow ever-more depressed and withdrawn, and taking to the bottle. On that summer's day, when some of his closest friends and collaborators were in the south of Sweden celebrating life and love, it all became too much for him. He decided to take his own life.

The shocking news reached Stig Anderson later the same day, but he decided to keep it to himself so as not to spoil the wedding party; everyone was finally told the morning after. As devastated as Stig was at losing a close friend of twenty years' standing, he also realized that with the passing of Bengt, Polar Music no longer had a record producer. He invited Björn into a rowing boat on a nearby lake so that they could talk

in private. Stig and Bengt had long groomed Björn to become a part of the Polar Music organization, and he now told Björn that he wanted him to start working as a producer at Polar, effective immediately. Björn, who felt that his partnership with Benny went above and beyond any other concerns, insisted that Stig had to hire Benny as well.

When Stig explained that he could only afford one producer, Björn found the perfect solution: hire both of them, he suggested, and let them split the salary. Cost-conscious Stig knew a favorable deal when he saw it and said yes. "It was a damned generous gesture on Björn's part," said Benny, who would always remember this touching manifestation of his and Björn's friendship. Over the next few years, they would gain plenty of varied experience in the recording studio, producing children's records, religious singers, big bands, and plenty more besides.

Stig Anderson had built a highly successful music business empire, not least through his acquisition of rights to foreign songs. But it was one thing importing hit tunes to Sweden. He felt that it must be possible to reverse the direction and sell Swedish songs to the rest of the world. Stig had realized that he had the perfect candidates in-house. "I could always see that

Björn and Benny had great ability as songwriters," he recalled at the height of ABBA's fame. "That was so evident. I knew they would be able to make a worldwide name for themselves as writers."

Despite the misgivings of music business colleagues both in Sweden and abroad—after all, with the exception of a number of opera singers, no Swedish songwriters or performers had ever managed a sustained international career—Stig refused to accept that it couldn't be achieved. But it wasn't until February 1972, when Björn and Benny's 1970 debut single, a song called "She's My Kind of Girl," was issued in Japan, of all places, that things started happening for real. The tune had the kind of melancholy tone to it that appealed to the Japanese. Upon release it shot to No. 1 on Japan's radio chart and peaked at No. 7 on the nation's sales chart, an exceptionally good result for a non-Japanese act.

This was the encouragement that Björn, Benny, and Stig needed. For a few years, Björn and Benny had been stuck in the Swedish light-pop/schlager field,

OPPOSITE The two couples become neighbors in Vallentuna, a suburb north of Stockholm

BELOW British group Blue Mink featuring singers Roger Cook (bottom, left) and Madeline Bell (bottom, center), c.1970

but they were really dreaming of going back to writing pop music in English, just like they'd done when they first met. Now they had the idea to write and record a bona fide English-language pop song, performing it together with their female companions. They had some inspiration from the band Blue Mink, on whose songs lead vocals were traded between Roger Cook and Madeline Bell. The band had several hits in the late 1960s and early 1970s, among them "Melting Pot," "Good Morning Freedom," and "The Banner Man." Why not try to do something similar?

On March 29, 1972, the group convened at Metronome Studio in central Stockholm and laid down a track called "People Need Love." With the male and the female halves of the group trading lines in the verses and coming together in the choruses, just like Blue Mink, the gospel-pop song—thematically aligning itself with early 1970s hits such as The New Seekers' "I'd Like to Teach the World to Sing," or any number of Blue Mink songs—marked a clear turning-point. Said Benny a couple of decades later, "I remember thinking, 'Now we've made our first really good record,' and I think Björn felt the same way."

The single was issued under the somewhat cumbersome name Björn & Benny, Agnetha & Anni-Frid, but "People Need Love" was, in effect, the first

ABBA recording. In the summer of 1972 it became a hit—a moderate one, but nevertheless a hit—prompting a change of direction for all concerned. Björn and Benny had been recording tracks for their second duo album, but most of those recordings were now scrapped in favor of an album together with Agnetha and Frida, with recording sessions beginning in the autumn of 1972.

The gods were clearly with them, as a potentially exciting opportunity for exposure came their way a few months into the album sessions. The track record of the songwriting team of Björn, Benny, and Stig was pretty good at this point, so, identified as potential hitmakers, they were now invited to submit a song for Melodifestivalen (the "Melody Festival"), the Swedish selection for the 1973 Eurovision Song Contest. In retrospect, it may seem odd that they were so excited by the prospect of entering Eurovision. After all, wasn't this competition the antithesis of everything they were striving to achieve—getting recognition as credible purveyors of contemporary pop music? But the reality of the matter was that they had very few alternatives if they wanted to reach out with their music outside Scandinavia. At this time, major record companies in Britain and America would say no to their music even before they'd heard it, so the thinking was that Eurovision would give them direct exposure to an audience of several hundred million viewers across Europe. If the song and the performance were strong enough, they would bypass the tastemakers and gatekeepers, their music being judged on merit alone, not on its geographical origin.

In early January 1973, Björn, Benny, and Stig took the boat out to the island of Viggsö in Stockholm's beloved archipelago to try to come up with the song. Stig had been the first to buy a house on the island, followed by Björn and Agnetha in 1971; two years later, Benny and Frida would follow suit. This island became the summer retreat for the entire ABBA "family," where they spent much time during ABBA's heyday.

Björn and Agnetha's property came with a small guest house with two bedrooms and an indoor porch, where there was just enough room for a piano, two chairs, and little else. This became a favorite songwriting retreat for Björn and Benny, as it offered them the peace, quiet, and splendid isolation necessary for them to be creative. Many ABBA songs were born in this cabin, among them classics such as "Dancing Queen" and "The Winner Takes It All."

Settled down on the porch in that cold January, Björn and Benny came up with a catchy melody. They played it for Stig, who agreed that it would be perfect

❝ I can still remember the chills and how the hair stood up on my arms. It really was something else. ❞

Michael B. Tretow

for Eurovision. Stig was a master at coming up with memorable titles that could be understood globally. After mulling things over for a bit, he settled on "Ring Ring" and wrote the Swedish lyrics very quickly. Just a few days later, on January 10, the group and their session musicians were back at Metronome Studio to record the song. It was an important session, not only because they hoped that this song would take them all the way to Eurovision.

A crucial individual in the ABBA story is their sound engineer, Michael B. Tretow. He was about the same age as Björn and Benny, and shared their enthusiasm at the prospect of making records that sounded like the best British and American output. Constantly searching for new sounds and exploring different ways

of recording, he was Björn and Benny's unofficial co-producer on the ABBA records and would play an essential part in making them sound so fresh even decades after they were first released.

At the time of the "Ring Ring" session Michael had just read a biography of American record producer Phil Spector, famous for his early 1960s wall-of-sound recordings with acts such as The Crystals, The Ronettes, and The Righteous Brothers. The book revealed how Spector's sound had been created, with five guitars, three pianos, and two bass guitars playing simultaneously, making for a massive sound. Excited, Michael told the equally enthused Björn and Benny about his discovery and they agreed to try this recording approach on the "Ring Ring" session. They didn't quite have the financial resources of a Spector session, so instead of several guitarists crammed together in the studio, they went for a "budget" approach. They had one guitarist, one bass player, and one drummer, but they would each play exactly the same parts twice, the second part being overdubbed onto the first part.

Michael also added another ingredient: For the second backing track overdub, he changed the speed on the tape recorder just slightly, in fact rendering it

out of tune—not so much that you'd notice it, but just enough to widen the sound even more. The effect astounded them all. "It was like the roof was caving in, Björn and Benny were ecstatic," Michael recalled. "And I can still remember the chills and how the hair stood up on my arms. It really was something else."

On February 10, 1973, Björn & Benny, Agnetha & Anni-Frid performed "Ring Ring" at Melodifestivalen. It was a tense situation for more reasons than one: Agnetha was heavily pregnant with her and Björn's first child and was about to give birth at any moment. Everyone was worried, not least the Swedish television staff. "I wasn't too stressed out myself but everyone around me was more or less hysterical, especially one of the studio hostesses," Agnetha recalled. "On one occasion she happened to hear a child shriek, came storming down the corridor and yelled, 'Oh, my goodness, has it arrived?' She thought I'd had my baby in the middle of the television studio!"

OPPOSITE ABBA sound engineer, Michael B. Tretow
ABOVE ABBA performing "Ring, Ring" live at Melodifestivalen, the pre-contest to the Eurovision Song Contest, February 10, 1973, in Stockholm

The performance of "Ring Ring" went ahead as planned, without any children being born—a daughter named Linda arrived two weeks later, in a safe hospital environment—but the outcome was not what the group had hoped for. Although "Ring Ring" had been tipped as the favorite to win, the jury of people from various parts of the music business—performers, songwriters, music journalists, and so on—placed it third. No Melodifestivalen victory meant no ticket to Eurovision and no television exposure to all those European countries. Doom and gloom prevailed in the group's dressing room afterwards; a furious Stig Anderson would never forget his wrath at the jury of experts who had deprived him and his group of the victory that he felt was rightfully theirs.

However, when "Ring Ring" was released as a single in Sweden, Stig and the group were vindicated in a way they could hardly have dared hope for. "Ring Ring" and the album of the same name—the first ABBA album, although it was credited to Björn & Benny, Agnetha & Frida ("Anni-Frid" became "Frida" on the records around this time)— were the biggest hits of 1973. On the combined singles and albums chart used in Sweden at the time, for two weeks in a row in April, the Swedish-language "Ring Ring" single was at No. 1, the English-language single at No. 2, and the album at No. 3.

Ring Ring was quite a patchy album, showing signs of having been cobbled together quickly once it was clear that the LP needed be issued sooner rather than later. The easy-listening ballad "I Am Just a Girl," for instance, was a reused backing track for a flop single Björn, Benny, and Stig had written for another artist. The not very rocky "Rock'n Roll Band" featured a rejigged backing track from a Björn & Benny single issued in Japan. But all in all, *Ring Ring* achieved what the group was aiming for at the time, which was to provide entertaining and easily digestible light-pop, with songs such as the singer-songwritery "Another Town, Another Train" and the perky "Nina, Pretty Ballerina" being as catchy as you could want. Notably, this was the only ABBA album that featured an Agnetha Fältskog songwriting contribution, "Disillusion," for which Björn wrote the lyrics. The male half of ABBA admired Agnetha's talents and encouraged her to submit more material to the group over the years, but self-doubt about her tunes stopped her. "I don't think they're good enough, quite simply, to be done by ABBA, so I guess it's some kind of self-criticism that holds me back," she admitted toward the end of the group's career.

It was only with the success of "Ring Ring" that the four members decided to make the group permanent and to focus all their energies on it. At the time, Björn and Benny were still expected to produce all kinds of acts for Polar Music, while Frida was still a solo performer recording for Polar, and Agnetha—tied to Cupol Records until the end of 1975 and "on loan" to Polar—also conducted a separate career. Over the next couple of years, however, all such commitments were phased out. What was originally a side project had become Björn, Benny, Agnetha, and Frida's main outlet as songwriters, musicians, and singers.

There was one crux that had to be resolved as soon as possible, though: their cumbersome name. Although it wasn't unheard of for a group to have a moniker based on the members' names, for audiences outside Scandinavia Björn & Benny, Agnetha & Anni-Frida didn't roll off the tongue quite as easily as, say, Crosby, Stills, Nash & Young. And since this Swedish band had their sights set on making it abroad, they simply had to come up with something else.

Stig Anderson, never the most patient of men, had long since tired of having to rattle off the four names when he was scribbling down internal memos in the office or talking to the media about them. Just for fun, he began referring to them as ABBA, the four letters in the name corresponding to each of the members' first names. Part of the joke was that there was a well-known canned fish factory in Sweden called Abba.

But although the name had been born in jest, Stig soon realized that it was actually quite good. A Gothenburg newspaper held a "think of a name for Björn & Benny, Agnetha & Frida" competition, but Stig's original suggestion prevailed. At first, the group weren't too happy about being known as ABBA: Not unreasonably, they felt it wouldn't be such a good idea if their music conjured up images of canned fish. Stig argued that this would only be the case in Sweden, and he pointed out that ABBA would be perfect for them— it was short and simple and could be pronounced by everyone across the globe. No one was able to come up with anything better, so the group finally admitted defeat. The canned fish factory was only too happy to lend its name to the group and sent them a box of canned tuna to celebrate the agreement.

But what about that international career they were shooting for? They failed to enter Eurovision, so was that the end of it? No—ABBA and Stig were not about to give up that easily.

OPPOSITE Agnetha and Björn welcome daughter, Linda, February 23, 1973

RING RING

SIDE ONE

Ring Ring (bara du slog en signal)
 [Swedish version]
Another Town, Another Train
Disillusion
People Need Love
I Saw It in the Mirror
Nina, Pretty Ballerina

SIDE TWO

Love Isn't Easy (But It Sure Is
 Hard Enough)
Me and Bobby and Bobby's Brother
He Is Your Brother
Ring Ring
I Am Just a Girl
Rock'n Roll Band

Recorded: Metronome, KMH, and Europa Film Studios, Stockholm, Sweden

Produced and arranged by: Benny Andersson and Björn Ulvaeus

Engineered by: Michael B. Tretow, assisted by Åke Eldsäter, Rune Persson, Lennart Karlsmyr, and Björn Almstedt

Personnel:
Agnetha Fältskog: vocals
Anni-Frid Lyngstad: vocals
Björn Ulvaeus: vocals, guitar
Benny Andersson: vocals, keyboards
Janne Schaffer, Bo Dahlman, Hasse Rosén: guitar
Rutger Gunnarsson, Mike Watson: bass
Ola Brunkert, Roger Palm, Derek Skinner: drums
Sven-Olof Walldoff: string arrangement

Cover art:
Peter Wiking: layout
Bengt H. Malmqvist: photography (front)
Lars Falck: photography (back)

Released: March 26, 1973 (UK release date: April 9, 1992; US release date: 1995)

Label: Polar POLS 242

Notes
International versions of the album featured a slightly different track list. The Swedish version of "Ring Ring" was removed, with the English version opening the album in its stead. The gap left by the English "Ring Ring" on side two was filled by "She's My Kind of Girl," Björn & Benny's Japanese Top Ten hit. "Ring Ring" itself featured lyrics by Neil Sedaka and his then songwriting partner Phil Cody, the first and only time that the group brought in outside help for their English-language lyrics.

3

AT WATERLOO
NAPOLEON DID
SURRENDER

At Waterloo Napoleon Did Surrender

I t was December 1973 and Stig Anderson was faced with a conundrum. Benny Andersson and Björn Ulvaeus had written a catchy up-tempo tune that he felt could be a hit, and it was up to him to come up with the words—that in itself was nothing out of the ordinary, as he had penned numerous lyrics for them over the past few years. In this case, however, the songwriting trio had been invited to submit a song for the following year's Eurovision Song Contest, scheduled to take place in Brighton, England, on April 6. And it was likely that this pop-rocker would be their contender.

But what should the lyrics be about, and, above all, what should the song be called? For Stig, the title was more important than anything: Once he had found a good, catchy title that was easy to remember and that could be easily understood in most countries, that was 90 percent of the work done. As he phrased it, "The title is the most important thing. It has to be short and quickly visible on the TV screen. It must be understandable in Poland and Yugoslavia as well."

The hook of the song required a trisyllabic word, which would also be its title, that much he knew. At one point he settled on "Honey Pie," but unlike Paul McCartney, who had successfully written and recorded a song with that title in 1968 for The Beatles' so-called *White Album*, Stig didn't feel sufficiently inspired to take it any further. Finally, as he leafed through a book of familiar quotations, he found those three syllables he was looking for: Wa-ter-loo. It was the name of a Belgian town which, through its connection to Napoleon Bonaparte's defeat by British and German forces at the battle near it in 1815, had come to symbolize defeat in general. Around this concept Stig

PAGE 48 ABBA, May 1974

OPPOSITE ABBA win the Eurovision Song Contest with their song "'Waterloo," Brighton, UK, 1974

> **"The title is the most important thing. It has to be short and quickly visible on the TV screen."**
>
> Stig

now quickly constructed a story about a protagonist surrendering to the love of a persistent suitor.

Before the end of 1973, the song had been recorded in the studio. Everyone agreed that this catchy tune would be the perfect contender for the Eurovision Song Contest. But just moments before Stig was heading for the airport and a Christmas holiday in the Canary Islands, he was given a demo tape of a brand-new song that Björn and Benny had written. Adorned with the working title "Who's Gonna Love You," it was more in line with a typical mid-tempo Eurovision ballad, the kind of entry that had won the contest in the past four years. Would this, perhaps, be an even better contender than "Waterloo"?

In the Canary Islands, Stig kept hearing the phrase "hasta mañana" all the time—and there was the perfect title for the new song. He dictated his lyrics down a crackly telephone line so that ABBA could go into the studio and finish the recording as soon as possible. With Agnetha on tear-soaked, Connie Francis-inspired lead vocals, the group knew that this was something that could work in Eurovision. After Stig returned home to Stockholm in early January, he reconvened with Björn and Benny at his home to make the final decision on which song to submit to Melodifestivalen, the Swedish selection. Should they go for "Waterloo," the song they were more excited about and which was how they wanted to present themselves to the world? Or would it be better to place their bets on "Hasta Mañana," which adhered more closely to the Eurovision format? They finally decided on "Waterloo." After all, winning was not the primary objective; it was more important to secure the exposure to hundreds of millions of television viewers. As Stig in particular was aware, some of the most famous songs to emerge from Eurovision, such as "Volare" (1958) and "Love Is Blue" (1967), had not been winners.

Leaving nothing to chance, the group was intent on making a splash in the contest. On Saturday, February 9, 1974, they appeared in Melodifestivalen dressed up in the most outrageous costumes that anyone had seen in that context. Inspired by glam rock acts such as T. Rex, Wizzard, and The Sweet, they had sought the help of a designer named Inger Svenneke, who had a boutique in central Stockholm, where

Benny and Frida used to shop from time to time. Shiny, colorful fabrics, epaulettes (fitting with the "military" theme), and platform boots combined to make up an ensemble that was guaranteed to make an impression on viewers. At Melodifestivalen, ABBA's energetic performance of "Waterloo" gave them a landslide victory—no "expert" jury this time, the music business people being replaced by a cross section of ordinary Swedes, spread throughout the country. ABBA's ticket to Brighton and Eurovision had been secured.

The opportunity to perform their song in front of millions of viewers was only half the victory, though. Stig Anderson knew that there was more to be done to achieve maximum impact. The day after the Melodifestivalen triumph, he hopped on a plane and traveled to several European countries, visiting the offices of ABBA's local licensees as well

CONGRESS
BAR ↓

as radio producers and disc jockeys, bringing with him promotional materials everywhere he went. Stig made it clear to everyone he met that ABBA were going to be seen across Europe in the Eurovision Song Contest on April 6, that they had a great, catchy song, and that they were going to be wearing eye-catching stage costumes—no one was going to be able to forget them. "You have the rights to 'Waterloo,' please see to it that it's available in the record shops in time for Eurovision," was the message. "Make the most of this exposure!"

OPPOSITE Arriving at Heathrow Airport, London, 1974
ABOVE ABBA at the Eurovision Song Contest, April 6, 1974, in Brighton, UK
OVERLEAF (L-R) Benny Andersson, Frida Lyngstad, Agnetha Fältskog, and Björn Ulvaeus, Stockholm, Sweden, after winning Melodifestivalen with "Waterloo," 1974

On the night of April 6, the Eurovision Song Contest took place at The Dome in Brighton. ABBA's performance of "Waterloo" was number eight in the lineup, sandwiched between two more typical Eurovision entries: Yugoslavia's melodramatic ballad and Luxembourg's perky oompah ditty. There could be little doubt: ABBA's glittery outfits and their almost rocky tune, with echoes of Wizzard's glam rock classic "See My Baby Jive," was like nothing ever seen or heard in the contest before. Going all the way in the gimmickry department, their conductor, Sven-Olof Walldoff, had even agreed to dress up as Napoleon.

Everything worked out exactly as they had hoped—and even better. Björn would recall being so nervous during the voting that he could barely watch it. Benny, cool as ever, watched the counting and, at a certain point, calmly concluded that no matter how the remaining juries voted, there was no way they were going to beat ABBA.

From the moment the evening's hostess, a nervously giggling Katie Boyle, announced that "Waterloo" was the winner, the rest of the night was like a blur for ABBA and their entourage. When accepting the songwriting award, Stig said the phrase "thank you" in a great number of languages, carefully rehearsed earlier in proceedings. His co-writers, meanwhile, were stopped by security guards who failed to realize that they were not only the performers but the writers as well: Benny managed to cut loose, but Björn never made it to the stage to receive the recognition he deserved. But it didn't really matter—the important thing was that they had won. After performing the song a second time, everyone, not least the media, wanted a piece of ABBA.

However, in the midst of the celebratory mood, a Swedish television news reporter had a somewhat different agenda. Even though ABBA were by far the most popular group Sweden had ever seen, their albums breaking all previous domestic sales records, there was also a strong anti-ABBA feeling in their home country. Their music was targeted for being crassly commercial, some commentators seemingly believing that music was a secondary concern for

Agnetha, Björn, Benny, and Frida. Clearly, Stig and ABBA must have a cynical formula that they applied so as to squeeze maximum profit from defenceless consumers, who had no choice but to helplessly submit to the group's seductive music.

That's why, on this night, the Swedish reporter cornered Stig and Frida and stated, "Last year you made a song about people phoning each other, this year you did a song about how 40,000 people died, cynically speaking." The hot-tempered Stig managed to control himself while the cameras were on, patiently explaining that Waterloo was a metaphor for defeat and, in the context of a mid-1970s pop song, had nothing to do with people dying on a battlefield 159 years earlier. Once the camera was turned off, he exploded: The reporter was told to "go to hell before an accident happens!"

But this was a minor blip on what was an otherwise wonderful night. They all knew that something big had happened to them, Agnetha crying with joy down the telephone line as she called her parents in Jönköping. "When I went to bed in the morning and everything around me was quiet," recalled Björn, "I thought to myself, 'My God, yesterday we were an unknown

group and tomorrow the whole world lies open for us. We've become famous overnight.'" Indeed they had. Stig's careful preparations meant that "Waterloo" shot to the top of the charts all over the planet, including a Top Ten placing in the United States and Top Five in Australia, both being countries where Eurovision meant absolutely nothing at the time. Those who study chart and sales statistics maintain that the "Waterloo" single was one of the top five global best-sellers of 1974, an

extraordinary result for a bunch of unknowns emerging from Scandinavia. Stig's theory had proved absolutely correct: The contest served as a platform for making the world aware that there was a group called ABBA and that they were very much able to write, produce, and perform commercially viable pop music.

"Waterloo" was, naturally, the title track on ABBA's second album, first released in Sweden on March 4, 1974. If *Ring Ring* had been a cobbled-together album—a handful of bona fide hits battling for space with remakes of earlier flop singles—*Waterloo* was made with a clear purpose from start to finish. That said, the group were still trying to find out who they were, which is part of *Waterloo*'s charm. Think of later masterpieces such as "Dancing Queen" or "The Winner Takes It All" and you can tell ABBA are in firm control of each and every piece of those recordings: Everything is in place and anything that might be superfluous to requirements has been removed. But on *Waterloo*, you

OPPOSITE AND ABOVE Posing for the cameras following their Eurovision success, 1974

have wobbly Mellotrons, squealy Minimoogs, a semi-trashy attempt at glam rock on "Watch Out," goofball lyrical conceits such as "King Kong Song," a free-form jazz guitar solo on "My Mama Said," and even a lead vocal from Benny on "Suzy-Hang-Around," the first and last time that happened on an ABBA record.

Today, Björn and Benny dismiss most of the album—Benny feels that "Waterloo," "Honey, Honey," and "Hasta Mañana" are the only truly good songs on it—and maintain that "Watch Out" and "King Kong Song" are among the worst things they ever recorded. Those of us who are not members of ABBA, however, can just enjoy the sense of discovery, the journey to what the group wanted to become, and at the same time get a generous serving of catchy, well-produced pop. For the tunes were already there, ABBA just needed to hone their craft—and while they were in the process of doing that, *Waterloo* would do just fine. At the time, record-buyers in Sweden certainly agreed, sending the album to No. 1: By the end of the year it had sold over 300,000 copies, more than any other album up to that point. It didn't do so well elsewhere, but still reached the UK Top Thirty, which, at the time, must have been rather good for a new band from the Northernmost parts of Europe.

After the Eurovision victory, everyone everywhere required a piece of ABBA. Television shows all over Europe wanted them as guests; newspapers, magazines, and radio wanted to interview them; teen mags wanted special photo shoots. Yet, incredible as it may seem, at this time, when the focus logically should be on ABBA only, the four members were still committed to projects that had nothing to do with the group. Frida was starting sessions for a Benny-produced solo album; Agnetha was kicking off her own solo album; and Björn and Benny had assignments as Polar Music house producers, including an album for The Hootenanny Singers, of which Björn, incredibly, was still a member. ABBA had also signed on for a summer *folkpark* tour in Sweden, with at least one gig planned for Denmark. And if that wasn't enough, before the summer was over they had to start writing and recording their next album. Unless Agnetha, Björn, Benny, and Frida wanted to end up with ulcers and nervous breakdowns, something had to give. After some discussion, they chose the tour as the one thing they could remove from the agenda.

Local promoters, who had looked forward to a lucrative attraction, were up in arms, as were the media. ABBA were letting down their Swedish audiences, wrote the papers, and a Danish promoter

even sent them an angry letter. "This is quite simply the biggest insult I've ever experienced during my many years in this business," he asserted. "I have engaged the biggest international stars and then I have to be ridiculed by a gang of Swedish amateurs, who have become too big because of a sudden hit and who are certain to be forgotten a year from now." From ABBA's point of view, they had been given a chance to establish themselves as an international hit act, and they were not going to let it slip out of their hands. "What were we supposed to do?" argued Björn. "Say 'no thank you' to all the offers and 'bye, bye, from now on we don't care that we won'?"

On a happier note, around this time ABBA enlisted the services of costume designer Owe Sandström for the first time. Over the next five years he would be their go-to person for anything that involved presentation for television promotion or live concerts. His first ensemble was among his most outrageous, with Björn looking like some kind of Prince-Valiant-meets-Superman-meets-The Sweet figure, Frida presented in a tight-fitting snakeskin costume, Benny in a relatively sane shiny blue jacket with feathers, and Agnetha in a bright-red and metallic bra-and-shorts outfit, exposing as much of her skin as possible.

These costumes, which set the tone for much of Sandström's future work for ABBA, were seen in the promo clip for a remixed version of "Ring Ring," issued as the follow-up to "Waterloo" in the UK (most other territories went with the *Waterloo* album's "Honey, Honey"). The remix—instigated by ABBA's British record company, CBS—added more electric guitar and some saxophone, so as to make it sound more like "Waterloo," but this revamp backfired on them: Following on from "Waterloo" spending two weeks at No. 1, "Ring Ring" stalled at No. 32. No doubt, ABBA's image as a Eurovision act didn't help, as their association with the contest immediately became a millstone around their necks, particularly in the UK, where everything they released over the next year or so would flop. The November 1974 single, "So Long," didn't even chart, while the June 1975 release, "I Do, I Do, I Do, I Do, I Do," climbed to No. 38, before falling off the charts. In Continental Europe, ABBA still had credible hits, but the message from UK media and record-buyers seemed to be, "Congratulations on winning the Eurovision Song Contest but we actually don't want to hear from you again."

It galled the group, particularly Björn and Benny, who saw the UK as the home of pop music: After all, this was where their idols, The Beatles, hailed from. It was also important to be successful in the UK if you wanted to be taken seriously in other markets. Björn maintains that the record company's declining faith in them manifested itself quite literally: For every visit they made to the UK, they were provided with a gradually less classy car and put up in a gradually less classy hotel. "I really remember it as a struggle against all these forces that were trying to hold us back during that period," he said many years later.

However, while ABBA were occupied with overcoming this British opposition, in another part of the world interest in their music was just about to reach stratospheric heights—and then some.

BELOW ABBA perform for German TV following their Eurovision win, Hamburg, May 1974

WATERLOO

SIDE ONE

Waterloo [Swedish version]
Sitting in the Palmtree
King Kong Song
Hasta Mañana
My Mama Said
Dance (While the Music Still Goes On)

SIDE TWO

Honey, Honey
Watch Out
What About Livingstone?
Gonna Sing You My Lovesong
Suzy-Hang-Around
Waterloo [English version]

Recorded: Metronome Studio, Stockholm, Sweden

Produced and arranged by: Benny Andersson and Björn Ulvaeus

Engineered by: Michael B. Tretow

Personnel:
Agnetha Fältskog: vocals
Anni-Frid Lyngstad: vocals
Björn Ulvaeus: vocals, guitar
Benny Andersson: vocals, keyboards
Christer Eklund: saxophone
John "Rabbit" Bundrick: keyboards
Janne Schaffer: guitar
Rutger Gunnarsson, Per Sahlberg: bass
Ola Brunkert: drums
Malando Gassama: percussion
Sven-Olof Walldoff: string arrangement

Cover art:
Ron Spaulding: layout
Ola Lager: photography

Released: March 4, 1974 (UK release date: May 17, 1974; US release date: July 1974)

Label: Polar POLS 252

Notes
International versions of the album removed the Swedish version of "Waterloo," using the English version as the opening track. Some countries released *Waterloo* as an eleven-track album, while others featured "Ring Ring" as the final track on side two. In most cases, the original 1973 version could be found there, but in North America a 1974 remix unique to that territory was featured.

BIGGER THAN
ANYTHING

Bigger Than Anything

In the UK, the BBC's *Top of the Pops*, with its strange mix of variety television aesthetics, reassuringly familiar middle-of-the-road performers, and sometimes provocative new pop and rock acts, was an integral part of the nation's pop culture. Considering the success of the format, it is somehow surprising that more countries did not try to introduce something similar, or if they did, it didn't quite have the same kind of impact.

There was a notable exception in Australia, where a show called *Countdown* was launched in 1974. Hosted by Ian "Molly" Meldrum, this highly popular show featured songs that had the potential to become hits and also a countdown of the week's Top Ten on the charts. Because of Australia's geographical location, however, and unlike *Top of the Pops*, *Countdown* couldn't rely on personal appearances by international hit acts. Inevitably, then, the show featured a high quota of so-called promo clips, what would become known as videos in the 1980s MTV era.

In July 1975, ABBA's "I Do, I Do, I Do, I Do, I Do" entered the lower region of the Australian charts. So far, the group's career down under had pretty much mirrored their fortunes in the UK, scoring a Top Ten hit with "Waterloo" but not enjoying much success since then, probably being regarded as little more than a one-hit wonder. There was something about this new song, however, and when it began taking off locally in Brisbane, the *Countdown* producers felt they should feature it on the show. ABBA's Australian record company, RCA, was contacted and asked if there was a promo clip available. There was—and not only for that song, but for three others from the group's current, eponymous album, *ABBA*.

The group had started producing promo clips purely out of necessity, the thinking being that it would spare them long and arduous journeys to faraway places such as the United States. A promotional trip to a European country was one thing, but anything beyond that required more of an effort. Also, Agnetha and Björn had been shocked when they arrived home after a long stretch of "Waterloo" promotion in April 1974 and their one-year-old daughter, Linda, didn't recognize them. Agnetha was particularly distressed by the experience, recalling how Linda "became shy and scared and stretched her hands out towards the nanny instead." Linda's parents vowed that in the future they would never be away for longer than two weeks;

PAGE 62 Frida (L) and Agnetha (R) pose with a kangaroo, March 1976, Australia
OPPOSITE ABBA, London, 1975
RIGHT ABBA picnicking in Sweden, 1974

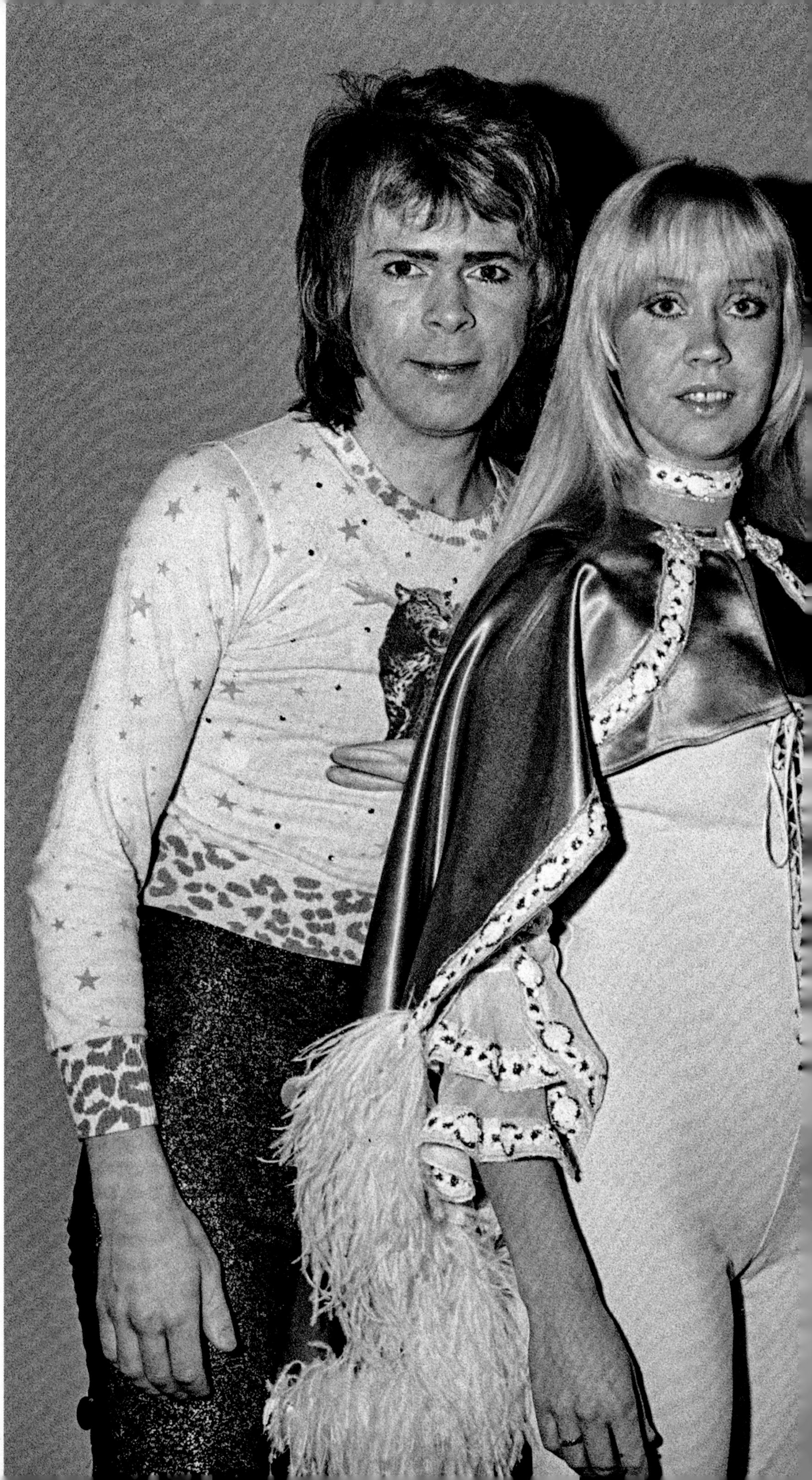

Backstage
at a show in
Copenhagen,
Denmark,
January 1975

> **If you listen to it, you will hear that there's no-one on it who's just strumming along; it's extremely tightly arranged: everybody's playing exactly what they're supposed to be playing.**
>
> Benny

RIGHT Benny backstage at the The Folkpark Tour 1975, Västervik, Sweden

BELOW Lasse Hallström, who would go on to direct *ABBA—The Movie*

for Agnetha the conflict between wanting to be with her children and the promotional commitments to ABBA would never be entirely resolved.

But how to balance the need for ABBA to promote their music with their wish to remain in Sweden? It was thought that promo clips could be part of the solution. ABBA enlisted up-and-coming director Lasse Hallström to produce these short films for them, starting with "Waterloo" and "Ring Ring" in the summer of 1974. With few exceptions, Hallström would direct all of ABBA's clips. Although he was never allowed much of a budget by the cost-conscious Stig Anderson, Hallström would usually overcome those restrictions, managing to conjure up some kind of visual excitement with the aid of various cinematic tricks and clever editing. As the director himself admits, the clips look rather old-fashioned today, but most of them have retained their charm, functioning as musical postcards from the 1970s. Parallel with his work for ABBA, Hallström would emerge as one of the most commercially successful film directors in Sweden, culminating with the 1985 film *My Life as a Dog*, which became his ticket to a career in Hollywood.

In the spring of 1975, Lasse Hallström had directed clips for four songs off their third album: "Mamma Mia," "SOS," "Bang-A-Boomerang," and "I Do, I Do, I Do, I Do, I Do." These were now sent to the *Countdown* people, who certainly liked "I Do, I Do, I Do, I Do, I Do" but were even more excited by "Mamma Mia." The song was clearly super-catchy and the clip exposed Agnetha and Frida as two dolls dressed up in Owe Sandström's glammy costumes—a body-hugging jumpsuit for Agnetha, a risqué miniskirt made up of teasingly revelatory strips of cloth for Frida—while Björn and Benny contentedly played away on their guitar and piano in the background.

At the time, however, Polar had no immediate plans to release "Mamma Mia" as a single. After getting positive feedback from the "I Do, I Do, I Do, I Do, I Do" clip, *Countdown* decided to screen "Mamma Mia" anyway. The reaction was explosive: A great number of Australians descended on record stores, wanting to buy the "Mamma Mia" single, only to be told that no such artifact was available. Polar had earmarked "SOS" as the next ABBA single, but after some discussions RCA were finally allowed to release "Mamma Mia." What happened next stands as one of those sensational stories in the history of recorded music, on a par with The Beatles occupying the top five positions on the US singles chart back in 1964.

In October 1975, after three months on the Australian charts, "I Do, I Do, I Do, I Do, I Do" finally hit the top spot, remaining there for three weeks before being replaced by "Mamma Mia," which spent a mind-blowing ten weeks at No. 1. Meanwhile, "SOS" was also released as a single and, after hovering at No. 2 for several weeks, followed "Mamma Mia" to the No. 1 spot, where it remained for one week. In total, an ABBA single had been at the top of the charts for fourteen consecutive weeks. Just a few months earlier, the group had seemed to be a one-hit wonder, and now they were suddenly bigger than anything previously seen in Australia.

No one has been able to satisfactorily explain why ABBA became so huge so rapidly in Australia in particular. The nation was regarded as fairly conservative at this time, and ABBA's non-threatening, suburban two-couples image may have helped. One catchy hit after another being released as singles in quick succession, and receiving prominent exposure on *Countdown*, certainly played their part. Finally, timing and luck—that delicate moment when record company, audience, and media happen to decide they're excited about the same thing at the same time—would have sealed the deal.

The three No. 1 singles were all available on ABBA's third album, simply entitled *ABBA*, which also became a runaway success in Australia, spending a total of eleven weeks at No. 1. First released in Sweden in April 1975, it was a huge hit in ABBA's home country as well, breaking the sales records set by the *Waterloo* album. With this new album, the group had taken further steps toward the classic ABBA sound they would be remembered for. Björn sang lead on only two songs, with the girls dominating the rest of the tracks, as they and the male half of the group agreed they should. There were still one or two slight missteps, such as the Björn-led funk attempt "Man in the Middle": As Benny determined retrospectively, "There's no groove in it whatsoever, although there was supposed to be," which was certainly a damning verdict for a track that aspired to be funky.

But masterpieces such as "Mamma Mia" and "SOS" went a long way toward obscuring whatever weaknesses the album may have contained. "SOS," featuring a compelling Agnetha lead vocal, established her as the group's prime exponent of heartbreak and utter desolation. It didn't matter so much if the lyrics were not very profound, for Agnetha had a way of making you believe every single word she sang. "Mamma Mia," meanwhile, featuring one of those magically forceful joint leads from both women, was perhaps the song that set the template for ABBA's future production

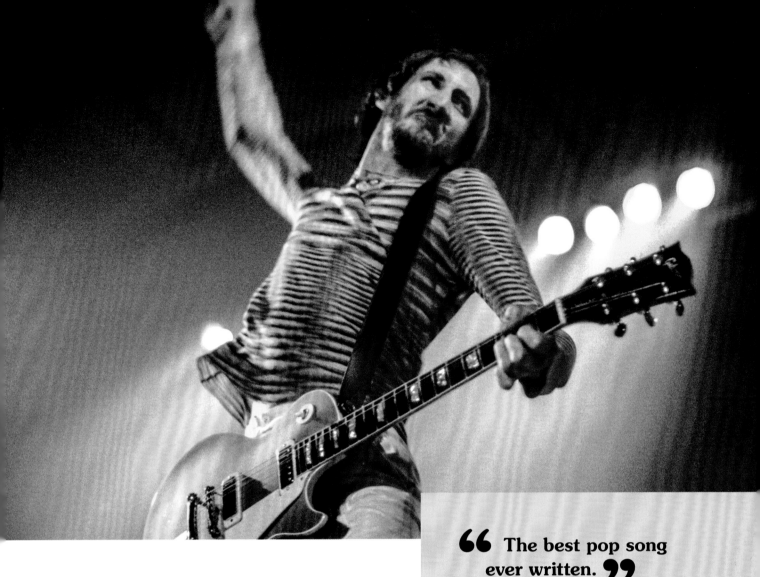

> **"The best pop song ever written."**
>
> Pete Townshend on "SOS"

work. "If you listen to it," Benny pointed out many years later, "you will hear that there's no-one on it who's just strumming along; it's extremely tightly arranged: everybody's playing exactly what they're supposed to be playing." On previous ABBA albums there had been greater freedom for the musicians, but from this moment on Björn and Benny would have a tighter grip on the reins. Benny would remember the experience of recording "Mamma Mia," the way each and every part of the musical construction had a clearly defined function, as a "eureka moment."

Parallel with ABBA's explosive rise in Australia, things were also starting to look a lot better in the UK, the group's post-Eurovision slump there being their biggest headache. British reviewers remained suspicious throughout 1975, damning "I Do, I Do, I

OPPOSITE Björn and Agnetha holding discs commemorating sales of their third album, *ABBA*, in Copenhagen, Denmark, May 1975

ABOVE Self-confessed ABBA fan Pete Townshend of The Who, pictured in 1975

Do, I Do, I Do" as "so bad it hurts," but with the release of "SOS" in September things were starting to look up again. The reviews still veered between begrudgingly respectful and outright bad, but crucially, for the first time since "Waterloo," ABBA had a song that the public responded to, no matter what the critics said. "SOS" reached No. 6, and a while later "Mamma Mia" finally brought the group back to No. 1 again. Commentary around that time also showed that the UK music press was recognizing ABBA as more than your usual flash-in-the-pan Eurovision act—as unlikely as it may have seemed, these four Swedes were actually expert producers of quality pop. Their fellow musicians noted much the same: Heavyweight rocker Pete Townshend from The Who was knocked out flat by "SOS" and would later tell a startled Björn that it was "the best pop song ever written," going on to extol its virtues in several interviews and writings over the years.

In international terms, the *ABBA* album was doing a lot better than the group's previous two albums, but it was still nothing compared to their next LP release. It all began in the Netherlands, where a compilation album entitled *The Best of ABBA*, featuring selections from the first three albums, was issued in August 1975. This prompted a release of the album in West Germany, while France followed suit with a similar collection entitled *Greatest Hits*. When import copies of *The Best of ABBA* found their way to Sweden, Polar rush-released their own *Greatest Hits* collection in November 1975. Around the same time, a similar album, *The Best of ABBA*, was released in Australia. In the course of 1976, labels in many other countries issued their own versions of these collections, which, except for a few minor variations, featured the same tracks.

The success of the *Greatest Hits*/*The Best of ABBA* compilations was nothing less than extraordinary. Most of the European releases charted very highly, in some countries being among the best-selling albums of 1976. The Australian version of *The Best of ABBA* sold more than a million copies, breaking all previous sales records. When the UK issued its version of *Greatest Hits* in the spring of 1976, it became the best-selling album of the year and would eventually be the nation's second-best-selling album of the decade, surpassed only by Simon & Garfunkel's *Bridge over Troubled Water*. Most importantly, with these collections ABBA had established themselves as an act that could sell albums.

The Australian sales were helped immensely by the group's first visit down under, in March 1976. The promo clips, intended to make such trips unnecessary, had backfired on ABBA—they had become such a phenomenon that RCA and everybody else demanded their presence. The group finally agreed when a deal was made to produce a television special, entitled *The Best of ABBA*, recorded in Sydney. They also visited Melbourne: Agnetha and Frida would never forget how their eyes filled with tears when a large number of fans greeted them on their arrival there. It was a physical manifestation of adulation, the kind of which they had never quite experienced before. As for the television special, it was a fairly unremarkable presentation with very little in terms of production values, but for the ABBA-craving Australians it was enough that Agnetha, Björn, Benny, and Frida had made the effort to travel so far to perform especially for them. When it was broadcast, *The Best of ABBA* reportedly broke all previous viewer records, famously exceeding the figures for the 1969 Moon landing.

One of the songs performed in the television special was ABBA's brand-new single, the Frida-led, Latin-tinged ballad "Fernando." Originally recorded in Swedish for Frida's Benny-produced 1975 solo album, *Frida ensam* ("Frida Alone"), it was decided at an early stage that it should be released as an ABBA track as well. Stig Anderson's original Swedish lyrics, about a heartbroken man and woman comforting each other, were supplanted by Björn's English interpretation, where the couple were looking back at the time when they were fighting in the Mexican Revolution.

Unsurprisingly, it too was a record-breaking release, spending fourteen consecutive weeks at No. 1 in Australia in 1976, a statistic matched only by The Beatles' "Hey Jude." Indeed, with six million copies sold globally, it would remain ABBA's biggest single for the rest of their active career. It was one of those songs, like Wings' "Mull of Kintyre" the following year, that attracted all generations: poppy enough for the youngsters yet harking back to old-style popular music in a way that felt familiar to their grandparents.

Where just a year earlier it had looked as if ABBA's success would be limited to a handful of countries in Continental Europe, being regarded as Eurovision has-beens in an important market such as the UK, they had turned their fortunes around. By mid-1976, they were one of the biggest acts on the planet. Many critics remained skeptical, but just as ABBA had managed to bypass such obstacles by using Eurovision as a platform, they had now reached the point where every new single, every new album was big news, and their reassuringly melodic and well-produced music appealed to a large slice of the audience. If there were critics that didn't like them, it just didn't matter very much, for the majority of their audience weren't necessarily *New Musical Express* readers.

ABBA were huge—and they were just about to become even bigger.

OPPOSITE ABBA, Stockholm, Sweden, April 1976

ABBA

SIDE ONE

Mamma Mia
Hey, Hey Helen
Tropical Loveland
SOS
Man in the Middle
Bang-A-Boomerang

SIDE TWO

I Do, I Do, I Do, I Do, I Do
Rock Me
Intermezzo No. 1
I've Been Waiting for You
So Long

Recorded: Metronome Studio, Glenstudio, and Ljudkopia Musikstudio, Stockholm, Sweden

Produced and arranged by: Benny Andersson and Björn Ulvaeus

Engineered by: Michael B. Tretow

Personnel:
Agnetha Fältskog: vocals
Anni-Frid Lyngstad: vocals
Björn Ulvaeus: vocals, guitar
Benny Andersson: vocals, keyboards
Janne Schaffer, Finn Sjöberg, Lasse Wellander: guitar
Rutger Gunnarsson, Mike Watson: bass
Ola Brunkert, Roger Palm: drums
Bruno Glenmark: trumpet
Ulf Andersson: saxophone
Sven-Olof Walldoff: string arrangement
Björn J:son Lindh: string and horn arrangement

Cover art:
Ron Spaulding, Sten-Åke Magnusson: layout
Ola Lager: photography

Released: April 21, 1975 (UK release date: June 7, 1975; US release date: August 28, 1975)

Label: Polar POLS 262

Notes

According to photographer Ola Lager, the sleeve concept, which featured ABBA drinking champagne in the back of a Rolls-Royce, was meant as an ironic commentary on the heavy criticism directed at the group in Sweden, where some felt that they were the commercial Antichrist.

GREATEST HITS

SIDE ONE

SOS
He Is Your Brother
Ring Ring
Hasta Mañana
Nina, Pretty Ballerina
Honey, Honey
So Long

SIDE TWO

I Do, I Do, I Do, I Do, I Do
People Need Love
Bang-A-Boomerang
Another Town, Another Train
Mamma Mia
Dance (While the Music Still Goes On)
Waterloo

Cover art:
Rune Söderqvist: layout
Hans Arnold: drawing
Bengt H. Malmqvist: photography

Released: November 17, 1975 (UK release date: March 26, 1976; US release date: August 24, 1976)

Label: Polar POLS 266

Notes

The many different variations of the albums titled either *Greatest Hits* or *The Best of ABBA*, issued in 1975, featured a selection of tracks from the same pool of fourteen songs. When "Fernando" was released as a single in 1976, some countries reissued the album with this track added. In the UK and the US, where *Greatest Hits* wasn't released until 1976, "Fernando" was always on the track list.

NIGHT IS YOUNG
AND THE
MUSIC'S HIGH

Night Is Young And The Music's High

In his 2018 book, *Nothing Is Real*, music journalist David Hepworth presents a list of *Five Records That Always Work at Weddings*. Places two to five in his list are occupied by up-tempo selections from Madonna, Bruce Springsteen, David Bowie, and House of Pain. And at number one? Why, ABBA's "Dancing Queen," of course. "There isn't a person in your room that doesn't love this record," asserts Hepworth, "plus it's just cheesy enough for the men to convince themselves they're somehow dancing satirically."

Whether the moves come attached with satire or not, "Dancing Queen" has certainly become one of those songs that are almost guaranteed to bring people out on a dance floor. However, no one is more surprised by this than ABBA's very own Björn Ulvaeus. "I don't really understand that," he once commented, "because for me the song is too slow to be a disco number." Björn had a point. The "Dancing Queen" tempo is somewhere around 100 bpm (beats per minute), whereas the ideal dance track should probably be at least 110 bpm. What brings people out on the dance floor, when they hear Benny's first piano roll, is rather the celebratory feel of the song and its uplifting spirit: You want to move to it at the same time as you're singing along to the chorus. After all, the lyrics are all about the here and now, escaping from everyday routines to enjoy your moment in the dance floor spotlight.

"Dancing Queen" was first released as a single in August 1976, but by that time it had been a full year since recording of the song began. In fact, the making of "Dancing Queen" can stand as an example of

PAGE 78 Waving to fans as they arrive at Tullamarine Airport in Melbourne, March 6, 1977

OPPOSITE Agnetha onstage at the Odeon Theatre, Birmingham during ABBA's first concert in Britain, February 10, 1977

"There isn't a person in your room that doesn't love this record."

David Hepworth

ABBA's meticulous craft and the lengths they would go to just to ensure that their recordings were the absolute best they could achieve at any given point.

The birth of an ABBA song would begin with Björn and Benny sitting down with an acoustic guitar and a piano, attempting to come up with strong tunes. These songwriting sessions would usually take place in the cabin on Viggsö island, or in the homes of Björn and Benny. The two songwriters would spend hour upon hour throwing melody fragments at each other, trying to recognize when something good came up. Usually, it would take days, sometimes weeks, before they had put together a tune they felt happy with. During this process they'd be singing random English phrases, just to have some words to carry the tune while they were working. The working titles of the songs were often taken from these preliminary "lyrics." "SOS," for instance, was originally entitled "Turn Me On," while "The Story of My Life" would transform into "The Winner Takes It All." In the case of "Dancing Queen," its working title was "Boogaloo."

The next step was to bring the tune to the recording studio, still without any final lyrics: At this stage, it was still just a melody. Together with session musicians on drums, bass, and electric guitar, an instrumental backing track would be worked out. In this process, the tunes would sometimes go through an endless variety of arrangements. One and the same song could be tried as a tango, a disco number, a ballad, or a 1950s-style rocker. It was all about keeping an

open mind, not leaving anything to chance, and not jumping on the first arrangement idea that popped into their heads.

The recording of a backing track would usually take one day, and after that there would perhaps be a few overdubs, usually of Benny's keyboards. At this stage, Björn would take home a rough mix of the backing track and listen to it over and over again, trying to figure out what the lyrics should be about. "A song or a piece of music has its own inherent language and story," he once explained. "It's in there somewhere, you just have to listen: 'What is it telling me?' The music and the lyrics will fit together in a special way if you can make that happen." In the first half of ABBA's career, Stig Anderson would often help them with the lyrics. Stig was especially good at coming up with catchy titles. He was the brains behind the title "Dancing Queen," while the actual lyrics were completed by Björn.

With the words written, the next step was to bring Agnetha and Frida to the studio to record the vocals. Far from being puppets that just did as they were told, both women played an active part in working out the vocal arrangements. "I know that I have contributed lots of ideas for arrangements, harmony parts, gimmicks, and solutions to several problems over the years," Agnetha explained at one point. Frida agreed. "Creativity is something that works really well when you're in a studio environment. We'd sing along to the piano or sometimes to the tape with the backing track. When you kept hearing the melody over and over, and you'd be working on it, other things would emerge, like little choir bits or a 'response.'" The recording of the vocals—lead parts as well as interminable overdubs of harmony parts—would usually be completed in one day. Impossible as this may sound, they could accomplish that much in such a short space of time because Agnetha and Frida worked hard and energetically in the studio.

At this stage, with the backing track, some overdubs, and the vocals in place, the next step was to see if there were any "holes" in the soundscape that could be filled and make the recording even more compelling. Usually there were. ABBA engineer Michael B. Tretow would almost tear his hair out by the roots in frustration as Benny had another idea and then another idea for keyboard overdubs, long after the twenty-four tracks available to them at the time had been filled. Michael then had to combine tracks—say, the drums, which may originally have occupied eight tracks—mixing them down to two or three tracks, in order to free up space on the tape for the overdubs. "Concepts like 'finished' or 'complete' are unknown to Benny," Michael sighed. "If he had his way, he would work on a song forever, because he just keeps coming up with new ideas all the time."

The overdubs would often be made parallel with the mixing, because during the process of combining the twenty-four tracks to the stereo master that record-buyers would hear, it would become apparent what was missing from the recording. The ABBA members would shake their heads in disbelief at the many contemporary critics who were convinced that the group were working according to some kind of formula, when in fact the songwriting and recording were intuitive processes, their gut feelings being their only guidelines.

Even with the knowledge of ABBA's ambitious standards, "Dancing Queen" was subject to an unusual amount of reworking in the studio. For instance, those descending piano chords in the intro of the song, today such an integral part of the recording, were only added very late in the process. Also, "Dancing Queen" originally started with a verse that was completely deleted from the recording, and the verse that we are used to as hearing as the first verse— "Friday night and the lights are low"— originally appeared much later in the recording and was edited out of the tape and moved to the start of the song. Small wonder that it took about five months before "Dancing Queen" was finally finished.

OPPOSITE Björn and Benny in the conference room at the Polar Music offices, trying to come up with new songs

ABOVE Frida (L) and Agnetha (R) rehearse "Dancing Queen" ahead of a gala to celebrate the marriage of Sweden's King Carl XVI Gustaf and future Queen, Silvia Sommerlath, Royal Swedish Opera, Stockholm, 1976

The song was ready for release around the same time as "Fernando," in early 1976, but ABBA held off on issuing "Dancing Queen" until August of that year, letting "Fernando" run its course on the world's charts first. In the meantime, "Dancing Queen" would be performed on television on a number of occasions, most spectacularly at a televised grand gala at The Royal Swedish Opera in Stockholm on June 18, the evening before the marriage of Sweden's King Carl XVI Gustaf and future Queen, Silvia Sommerlath. On a roster dominated by opera performers, ABBA was the only modern pop act to appear at that prestigious event. It was the King himself, a bit of a nightclubber in his bachelor days and perhaps not really an opera fan, who had requested that ABBA should appear at the gala.

When "Dancing Queen" was finally released, it shot to No. 1 most everywhere—it would almost be easier to list the countries where it didn't peak at the summit.

Notably, "Dancing Queen" gave ABBA their first and only chart-topper in the United States, a country where they had several hits and decent album sales, but never quite achieved the stratospheric success they enjoyed elsewhere. With time, the jubilant feeling of "Dancing Queen" would turn it into ABBA's most famous song: It was the recording people would point to as the prime example of the songwriting and production expertise of Björn and Benny, and, not least, Agnetha and Frida's hallmark high-energy, full-force vocals.

The "Dancing Queen" single was the first taster from ABBA's fourth album, *Arrival*, issued in October 1976. The single and the album were also where most people saw the famous ABBA logo with the backwards B for the first time. The logo had been designed by Rune Söderqvist, the man behind every ABBA album sleeve from 1975's *Greatest Hits* to *ABBA Live* in 1986. After trying different variations for the logo, he finally found the right solution. Recalled Rune, "I suddenly realised

that 'this is how it must be, this is logical—these two couples belong together, and so each B should be turned towards each A.'" The logo was unusually clean and uncluttered, and as such something of an anomaly in the mid-1970s. In the long term, however, this turned out to work in its favor, as the classic shape of the logo ensured that it would never go out of the style in the ensuing decades.

If the previous three albums had presented a band on a journey, trying to figure out who they were, where their strengths and their weaknesses lay, then *Arrival* was the first ABBA album to offer a complete collection of all the qualities we love the group for today. They

ABOVE Björn poses with the album cover of *Arrival* featuring the now familiar ABBA logo

OPPOSITE (L-R) Frida, Björn and Agnetha of ABBA onstage in Denmark, February 1977

had abandoned most thoughts of trying to convince as an outright rock band: Although "Tiger" inclined toward rock, those tendencies were there to support what was essentially a pop song. The songwriting had also gone up a further few notches: There are simply no weak tracks on the album. ABBA had spent more hours than ever before in the studio, polishing and fine-tuning every recording until it was exactly like they wanted it.

The album pulled you in, from the crisp acoustic guitars on the first track, the joyful "When I Kissed the Teacher." It had three outstanding singles on it—"Dancing Queen," as well as two Frida-led tracks: the cabaret-tinged "Money, Money, Money" and the divorce classic "Knowing Me, Knowing You," with its powerful imagery of a quiet house that was once filled with the sounds of children playing. But almost every track on the album could have been a hit single.

But what about the light and bright "Dum Dum Diddle," the reader may ask. Doesn't the nonsensical title alone mark it as an example of everything that's wrong with ABBA? Not necessarily. Certainly, lyricist Björn feels embarrassed about the song today—"It might as well have been [entitled] 'Dumb Dumb Diddle'!"—and his feelings are backed up by Frida, who once stated that it was "A silly song; I don't like it." However, although the title may have a strong bubblegum flavor, the song is in fact the same expertly executed catchy pop that marks the other tracks on the album. *Arrival* was, quite simply, the best pop that money could buy at the time. It was a major success everywhere, going on to become the UK's best-selling album of 1977.

As if to crown their recent achievements, in January 1977, ABBA embarked on a triumphant concert tour, its first European leg covering Norway, Sweden, Denmark, West Germany, the Netherlands, Belgium, and Britain. The last time they'd tried to wow audiences outside the Nordic countries, in November 1974, the experience had been anything but triumphant. An original, rather ambitious itinerary that included the UK

had been severely curtailed—partly because ABBA had an album to record at the time, but perhaps mainly because there wasn't yet enough demand for them as a concert attraction. A trek taking them on scattered dates in Denmark, West Germany, Austria, and Switzerland was marked by cancelled or less-than-sold-out shows and a rather tepid atmosphere. Björn would remember the tour as "completely miserable."

Two years later, the situation couldn't have been more different. For their two London shows in February 1977, ABBA had been thinking of booking Wembley Empire Pool but, burned by the 1974 tour, they were concerned that they might not be able to fill it, instead booking the much smaller Royal Albert Hall. They shouldn't have worried, as they famously received a reported 3.5 million ticket applications for the less than twelve thousand tickets available—to meet the demand ABBA would have had to play more than six hundred shows at this venue. The tour itself received mixed reviews from critics—some felt it was a bit clinical and mechanical, and, being rather family-friendly, not exactly what they

expected from a rock concert—but every show was sold out and audiences loved it.

The stage presentation was simple enough: a predominantly white stage, decorated with red roses. The suitably fantastical costumes, created by Owe Sandström and his tailor partner Lars Wigenius, were made up of various combinations of white and gold. This color scheme was arrived at on the basis of *The Girl with the Golden Hair*, the twenty-five-minute "mini-musical" performed on the tour. Björn and Benny had long been dreaming of writing a musical and now that they were going on tour, the plot they concocted—about a naïve young girl leaving her hometown to pursue a career in singing, only to find out that she's become trapped by fame—provided a flexible enough framework within which a few new songs could be performed. Sporting curly blonde wigs, Agnetha and Frida both played the part of the girl.

As for the wisdom of introducing this just slightly dark and disturbing work in the midst of a pop music stage show, Benny has expressed some retrospective

OPPOSITE AND ABOVE Onstage at the Royal Albert Hall, London, UK, February 14, 1977

doubt. "I suspect the whole thing was probably quite weird for the audiences: they just wanted to see ABBA," he told author Philip Dodd, adding that "it was not a good choice for a tour." Nevertheless, one of ABBA's best-loved songs, "Thank You for the Music," emerged from the mini-musical. The concert otherwise featured a selection of ABBA's string of hits up to this point, along with a number of album tracks, predominantly from *Arrival*: Eight of its ten songs were performed on the tour.

In March, the tour continued to Australia, the two weeks ABBA spent down under being unlike anything in the group's history. From the moment their plane touched down in Sydney, they didn't have a moment's peace. "The Australian tour was the most incredible of all the things that I experienced with ABBA," confirmed Agnetha many years later. "There was fever, there was hysteria, there were ovations, there were sweaty, obsessed crowds." In the year that had passed since they were last in Australia, ABBA had only grown bigger. Merchandise sales were exploding; every new

single they released went to No. 1; and older singles—even B-sides of previous hits—charted in the higher regions. They seemed to be on television all the time, with some so-called specials being cobbled together with promo clips linked together by sometimes not very inspired hosts.

This was the frenzied atmosphere ABBA entered into on their arrival. "There was ABBA—ABBA—ABBA—everywhere," recalled engineer Michael B. Tretow, who accompanied the tour. "There were pictures of them on every corner, wherever you went." Tretow was on the tour to record the concerts for a possible live album, but also for the soundtrack of a cinema release documenting the adventure, directed by Lasse Hallström.

ABOVE Sporting curly blonde wigs, Agnetha (L) and Frida (R) perform a mini-musical interlude during ABBA's Royal Albert Hall show

OPPOSITE Live onstage at Manchester Apollo, UK, February 1977

The tour as such got an ominous start when the first show, at Sydney Showground in front of more than twenty thousand people, almost had to be cancelled because of heavy rain, turning the outdoor venue to mud. But the concert was seen through after all, with stage hands—including ABBA manager Stig Anderson—frantically mopping up the water. Despite the danger of mixing electronics with water, and the risk of onstage electrocution, with the exception of Frida slipping and injuring a finger there were no serious incidents. After a second show in drier conditions the following day, the tour continued to Melbourne, where the group received an astounding welcome. All the way from the airport to the city, the streets were lined with people, waving and shouting to the group. They were taken straight to a reception at the Melbourne Town Hall, where they went out on the balcony to wave at thousands of cheering and screaming fans.

The Melbourne shows were followed by an outdoor concert in Adelaide, where one of the television channels had a five-minute slot every day that ABBA

was in Australia, giving updates on the progress of the tour. In conjunction with the show, there were continuous live radio reports during the hours leading up to the concert, some journalists having taken a helicopter to cover the event and give a bird's-eye view report of the proceedings.

The entourage traveled on to Perth for the final shows of the tour. In an attempt to escape the ever-present fans and media, they went out on a boat to get some peace. But even out at sea they weren't left alone: A television news crew managed to locate them and were rewarded with some awkward footage of a reluctant ABBA politely answering inane questions.

The pressure from the media was bad enough, but the overwhelming hysteria of the fans was something else entirely. Depending on which ABBA member you ask, it was either all part of the fun of being on such an adventure, or something decidedly darker. While Frida would recall some of the experiences as "nasty," Agnetha had a lot more to say on the subject. "Sometimes it was awful," she related in her 1996 memoir, *As I Am*. "I felt as if they would get hold of me and I'd never get away again. It was as if I was going to be crushed. On occasions they would grab hold of us in the most unpleasant ways, and there were times when we burst into tears once we were inside the cars."

If there was a hope that the concluding five shows in Perth, at the indoor Entertainment Centre, would be less dramatic, any such expectations were shattered at the first concert. There were only thirty minutes left of the show when the venue received a bomb threat. Everyone was ushered out of the building, and while Benny picked up his accordion and, together with some of the musicians, entertained the audience outside — they were separated from the audience by a fence— the venue was searched. Fortunately, it turned out that the threat had been a hoax, and after twenty minutes everyone went inside again to conclude the show.

Flying home after the Perth shows, feelings within the group varied greatly. Björn and Benny, perhaps more used to the intense pressure of hysterical crowds after their years as teen idols in the 1960s, took it all on the chin. Whatever inconveniences they may have suffered

in Australia, above all it had been a lot of fun. For the female half of the group, who as lead singers were the focal points of ABBA, emotions were more mixed. Frida, who had transformed from a restrained solo performer to a singer who loved being onstage, perhaps found it easier to relish the attention, as overwhelming and even frightening as it could be sometimes. For Agnetha, though, the tour would leave permanent scars. "No one who has experienced facing a screaming, boiling, hysterical crowd could avoid feeling shivers up and down their spine," she told author Brita Åhman in 1996. "It's a thin line between ecstatic celebration and menace. It can turn around in a flash. I don't think anyone could stay the same after such an encounter. It affects your personality. Something changes within you and it can be the source of phobias."

BELOW Björn and Frida perform "Why Did It Have To Be Me" during ABBA's tour of Australia, 1977

OPPOSITE Frida and Agnetha during the ABBA concert at the Sidney Myer Music Bowl in Melbourne, March 1977

ARRIVAL

ABBA /ARRIVAL

SIDE ONE

When I Kissed the Teacher
Dancing Queen
My Love, My Life
Dum Dum Diddle
Knowing Me, Knowing You

SIDE TWO

Money, Money, Money
That's Me
Why Did It Have to Be Me?
Tiger
Arrival

Recorded: Metronome Studio and Glenstudio, Stockholm, Sweden

Produced and arranged by: Benny Andersson and Björn Ulvaeus

Engineered by: Michael B. Tretow

Personnel:
Agnetha Fältskog: vocals
Anni-Frid Lyngstad: vocals
Björn Ulvaeus: vocals, guitar
Benny Andersson: vocals, keyboards
Janne Schaffer, Lasse Wellander,
Anders Glenmark: guitar
Rutger Gunnarsson: bass, string arrangement
Ola Brunkert, Roger Palm: drums
Lars O. Carlsson: saxophone
Sven-Olof Walldoff: string arrangement

Cover art:
Rune Söderqvist: layout
Ola Lager: photography

Released: October 11, 1976 (UK release date: November 5, 1976; US release date: January 4, 1977)

Label: Polar POLS 272

Notes

The title of the album was thought up by designer Rune Söderqvist's partner, Lillebil Ankarcrona, who felt that *Arrival* would be appropriate when the cover showed the group sitting in a helicopter. It also became the title of the instrumental track closing the album. In Australia and New Zealand, "Fernando," which hadn't been included on the local compilation *The Best of ABBA*, was squeezed in between "Why Did It Have to Be Me" and "Tiger" in the track list.

6

ACCEPTING THE
CONSEQUENCES

Accepting The Consequences

In the summer of 1977, Björn Ulvaeus found himself lying on the floor of the basement lounge in the house he and Agnetha shared at the time. Three years earlier, both ABBA couples had left the suburb of Vallentuna and its middle-class area of modest terraced houses, and they were now living in more stately homes on the island of Lidingö. Located just outside of Stockholm, Lidingö was at this time the celebrity's first choice.

Björn had chosen the basement lounge for a bit of seclusion as he was writing the lyrics for a new ABBA song, apparently feeling like he wanted to be lying down as he searched for the right words. The lyrics he came up with were for a compelling Frida-led ballad entitled "One Man, One Woman," one of the true masterpieces on ABBA's forthcoming album. The song depicted a marriage in trouble, some of the key lines being "no smiles, not a single word at the breakfast table" and "you leave and you slam the door".

Björn would always maintain that his lyrics were never truly autobiographical—but was there perhaps more than a grain of truth, of real-life experiences, embedded in "One Man, One Woman"? As he and Agnetha would later reveal, their marriage had been under severe strain at this time. They were developing in different directions as people, and however much they tried to reclaim common ground, it just became harder to reconcile their differences. When Agnetha fell pregnant with their second child in early 1977, they hoped this would help seal the cracks in the marriage. Perhaps tellingly, "One Man, One Woman" ends in a rather optimistic fashion: The husband returns home

from work and the couple conclude that "our love is a precious thing / worth the pain and the suffering / and it's never too late for changing." For now, that was pretty much how Agnetha and Björn tried to view their own real-life marriage.

"One Man, One Woman" was one of the songs on ABBA's fifth album, *ABBA—The Album*, sessions for which had been ongoing since the end of May 1977, following a bit of rest after the conclusion of the Australian leg of their tour. In June, they also had to set aside some days for completing scenes for the film released as *ABBA—The Movie* later in the year. Because of the chaotic nature of the tour, director Lasse Hallström didn't have quite the access to ABBA that he'd hoped for in Australia. This necessitated additional filming in Stockholm, which masqueraded as various Australian cities. One scene, showing the group reading reviews in an Australian hotel room, was in fact filmed at Stockholm's Sheraton Hotel.

Originally meant to be a 16 mm in-concert document of their tour, to be shown on television, the project had grown to a Panavision film for cinema release. Lasse Hallström felt that a straight-out concert film would test the patience of even the most diehard ABBA fan, so, to create some kind of cinematic forward motion, he concocted a plot about a hapless radio disc jockey chasing ABBA for an interview. Although it wasn't hard to understand why the director wanted to add a plot to the film, it has to be said that it's hard to feel much sympathy for the disc jockey as he chases the group across Australia. He comes across as both smug and stupid, and one feels that if he should end up not getting the interview he was craving, it seems unlikely the audience would shed many tears for his misfortune.

ABBA—The Movie received its world premiere in Sydney on December 15. The opening was attended by Stig Anderson, who, being almost as well recognized as the ABBA members themselves in Australia, was mobbed by hysterical fans. ABBA attended the Stockholm premiere on December 26. Reviews at the time were mixed, but viewed from the perspective of four and a half decades, and disregarding the annoying disc jockey, the film stands as an invaluable document of ABBA onstage. The concert scenes are great and show the group as a truly convincing and engaging live act with a cracking backing band, putting the lie to the concert reviews that had marked their stage show as clinical.

Released in tandem with the movie, *ABBA—The Album* presented a group that seemed keen to come across as ambitious. Up to and including *Arrival*, ABBA had taken a lot of flak for what was regarded as lightweight tunes and often insubstantial lyrics, whether they were entitled "King Kong Song," "Bang-A-Boomerang," or "Dum Dum Diddle." Björn took the

BELOW At the premiere of *ABBA—The Movie*, Stockholm, Sweden, December 1977
OPPOSITE American *ABBA—The Movie* poster

criticism of the lyrics to heart and decided that if he had to write them anyway, he might as well regard it as an interesting challenge rather than a chore to be got over with as quickly as possible.

ABBA—The Album marked a quite dramatic change in all departments. Out went teen-slanted pop confections such as Arrival's "When I Kissed the Teacher," to be replaced by philosophical semi-prog workouts in the vein of ABBA—The Album's opening track, "Eagle." The lead-off single, released in October 1977, was the laid-back "The Name of the Game," featuring an ambitious six-part structure, with those parts somehow tied together and made to interact with one another, helped along in no small way by Agnetha and Frida's lead vocals, trading parts one minute, blending into each other's vocal spectra the next. The three selections from the mini-musical unveiled on the tour earlier in the year also pointed forward. "Look," ABBA seemed to say, "we have ambitions beyond 'Waterloo' and 'Mamma Mia.' You may have tried to dismiss us as purveyors of the simplest kind of pop, but we can be serious when we want to." The song that would have reminded the ABBA fan most of the high-energy pop they had first fallen in love with was "Take a Chance on Me," the second single from the album and, perhaps tellingly, its biggest hit: Given a choice, this is what most record-buyers wanted from ABBA. Nevertheless, ABBA—The Album was a great commercial success, seemingly reaching No. 1 almost everywhere.

One notable exception was Australia, where the madness of the tour in March 1977 was followed by a dramatic drop in interest. It began when "Knowing Me, Knowing You" was released as a single in tandem with the tour, and, following six consecutive No. 1 hits, peaked at No. 9. Since the song was already available on the super-successful *Arrival* album, perhaps this wasn't so surprising. But when "The Name of the Game" was issued later in 1977, not being available on any album at that point, it only climbed to No. 6—and took three months to get there. Similarly, *ABBA—*

OPPOSITE Björn, Agnetha, and Frida at the London premiere of *ABBA—The Movie*, 1978
ABOVE ABBA and Keith Moon (center), 1978

The Album sold about 10 percent of what *The Best of ABBA* and *Arrival* had achieved, and never reached No. 1. One would have to look to The Bee Gees and their slump in the United States a few years later—two extraordinarily successful No. 1 albums, in the shape of the *Saturday Night Fever* soundtrack and *Spirits Having Flown*, were followed by *Living Eyes*, which got no further than No. 41—to find a comparable dramatic drop in popularity. Quite simply, the Australians had been force-fed ABBA in much too large portions, and after the intense insanity of the tour many of them decided that they'd had enough. ABBA and Stig Anderson had been concerned at the overexposure and done what they could to put a stop to it, but it was too little too late. During their active years, ABBA would never again have a No. 1 album or single in Australia.

ABBA, 1978 in Stockholm.
(L-R) Benny, Frida,
Agnetha, Björn

Around the time of *The Album* and *The Movie*, Björn and Agnetha's second child, a son named Christian, was born. The pregnancy had been a difficult one for Agnetha and at one point it looked as if the release of the album would have to be postponed as her doctor told her that she should be resting and certainly not be reaching for high notes in a recording studio. ABBA managed to work around this by installing a reclining chair in the studio so that Agnetha could be lying back in repose as she recorded her vocals. It was a sign of just how important a commercial proposition ABBA had become, and how much had been invested in the simultaneous launch of *The Album* and *The Movie*. "It was ABBA; the world was waiting for a new album," as Agnetha herself phrased it many years later.

Following the Scandinavian release of the film and the album, and after spending time with Christian for a couple of months, Agnetha joined in the promotional efforts for *ABBA—The Album*, which was issued in January or February 1978 in most countries. The most spectacular enterprise was the promotional campaign designed to make ABBA as big in the United States as they were in the rest of the Western world. So far, they had enjoyed a number of Top Twenty hits and one No. 1 in "Dancing Queen," but album sales were, if not exactly bad, then still not at the stratospheric levels in

countries such as Sweden, Australia, and the UK. It was a challenge that couldn't go unanswered.

Polar Music and Atlantic Records, ABBA's American record company, invested a substantial amount of money in a five-month promotional campaign, kicking off at the end of March. Employing the services of expert promoters the Scotti Brothers, May 1978 was designated ABBA Month in the United States. A huge billboard was erected above Sunset Strip in Los Angeles, proclaiming ABBA as "The largest selling group in the history of recorded music," a claim that may not have been entirely accurate but certainly sounded impressive. ABBA themselves spent a couple of weeks in Los Angeles, mainly to record a prime-time television special entitled *Olivia!*, where Olivia Newton-John was the main attraction, with ABBA and Andy Gibb co-starring.

The result was that "Take a Chance on Me" reached No. 3 on *Billboard*'s singles chart, ABBA's best-ever

ABOVE Agnetha and Björn welcome a son, Christian, on December 4, 1977

OPPOSITE Frida (L) and Agnetha (R) during rehearsals ahead of a performance on West German TV show *Star Parade*, May 1978

placing with the exception of "Dancing Queen," and *ABBA—The Album* peaked at No. 14, the group's highest-charting album. Yet, it wasn't the No. 1 success that everyone had hoped for, and it was questionable whether there had been enough payback from the investment made in the campaign. "It didn't kick the record like it should've, like it did in every other country," recalled Atlantic boss Jerry Greenberg.

Shortly before the campaign started, ABBA had begun sessions for their sixth studio album, eventually released as *Voulez-Vous*. It was to be their most difficult album yet. Under pressure, mainly from themselves, to develop and move forward, Björn and Benny found it difficult to come up with songs that felt like they belonged on a late-1970s pop album. Such was their punishing quality control at this stage that some songs might be fully recorded, but then thrown on the scrap heap because their gut feelings told them there was something wrong with the track. ABBA had hoped to have the album out before the end of 1978, but the uphill creative struggles—coupled with the group members allowing themselves an extended summer holiday for

the first time since ABBA came together—meant that there was little hope of record stores being able to offer a new album in time for Christmas. "I can tell from the look in Björn's eyes when he gets home how the day's work has been," said Agnetha at the time.

She also had other reasons to be concerned at the look in her husband's eyes. The birth of Christian, although a most welcome child, had not been enough to renew the spark in Björn and Agnetha's relationship. The couple sought help from a marriage counselor, but he could only confirm that they had reached the right conclusion about their life together. "When I found that I no longer wanted to go home in the evening and would try to delay it as late as possible, hoping that Agnetha would have gone to bed," Björn recalled, "then I knew I had to do something about it." Said Agnetha, "When you find that you've talked through absolutely everything and you still fail to get through to each other, then you must accept the consequences." The decision to end the marriage was made in the autumn of 1978, but the couple kept up a brave face to the outside world for a further few months.

OPPOSITE ABBA are pictured with Olivia Newton-John (front, right), Andy Gibb (back, left), and director Steve Binder (back, center) during rehearsals for the TV special, *Olivia!*, in Los Angeles, US, May 1978

ABOVE L-R: Michael B. Tretow, Björn Ulvaeus, bassist Rutger Gunnarsson, drummer Ola Brunkert, guitarist Lasse Wellander, and Benny Andersson during production of the *Voulez-Vous* album, 1978

RIGHT ABBA in London, UK, December 1978

In a strangely coincidental development, around the time that Björn and Agnetha decided on their breakup, the other half of the group were finally married. Benny and Frida had planned to marry many years earlier—Frida had even sewn a wedding dress for the occasion—but ABBA got in the way and the right time never seemed to present itself. But on October 6, 1978, they tied the knot in a simple, low-key ceremony in their local church on Lidingö. In fact, in an ultimately successful attempt to keep it from the media, the event was so low-key that not even Björn and Agnetha knew about it, the ceremony being attended only by the couple's children and their housekeeper. The following day, Benny and Frida had a party at their home, but maintained that they would have had that shindig anyway and that it had no relation to their wedding. After living together for nine years, perhaps the marriage wasn't a very big deal in the larger scheme of things, although naturally this ceremonial manifestation of their love was emotionally charged. "A ring doesn't mean anything in itself," said Frida. "[But] when you've got this close to each other, not completely without effort, it felt like a nice red-letter day. I was really touched throughout the entire wedding ceremony."

As for the new ABBA album, toward the end of the year, nine months after sessions began, they only had half the tracks they needed, three of which had been recorded in the final few months of the year—just a few years earlier they would have completed two LPs within that time frame. Clearly, there could be no Christmas

release of the album, which was pushed back to an unspecified date in 1979.

Capping a turbulent year, Björn, Agnetha, and their two young children spent Christmas Eve together as a family one last time (Christmas Eve being the important day in Swedish Christmas celebrations). The following day, Agnetha put the kids in her car and drove away to her new home on Lidingö. After ten years together, eight as husband and wife, Björn and Agnetha concluded their chapter of the ABBA fairy tale.

OPPOSITE Agnetha and Björn, Stockholm, Sweden, 1977
BELOW Frida and Benny appear on French TV show *Les Rendez-vous du dimanche* in April, 1978

66 **A ring doesn't mean anything in itself, [but] when you've got this close to each other, not completely without effort, it felt like a nice red-letter day. I was really touched throughout the entire wedding ceremony.** 99

Frida

ABBA— THE ALBUM

SIDE ONE

Eagle
Take a Chance on Me
One Man, One Woman
The Name of the Game

SIDE TWO

Move On
Hole in Your Soul
"The Girl with the Golden Hair"
 —3 scenes from a mini-musical—
Thank You for the Music
I Wonder (Departure)
I'm a Marionette

Recorded: Marcus Music, Metronome Studio, Glenstudio, Stockholm, Sweden, and Bohus Studio, Kungälv, Sweden

Produced and arranged by: Benny Andersson and Björn Ulvaeus

Engineered by: Michael B. Tretow

Personnel:
Agnetha Fältskog: vocals
Anni-Frid Lyngstad: vocals
Björn Ulvaeus: vocals, guitar
Benny Andersson: vocals, keyboards
Janne Schaffer, Lasse Wellander: guitar
Rutger Gunnarsson: bass, string arrangements
Ola Brunkert, Roger Palm: drums
Malando Gassama: percussion
Lars O. Carlsson: saxophones, flutes

Cover art:
Rune Söderqvist: layout, illustration
Björn Andersson: illustration
Barry Levine: photography

Released: December 12, 1977 (UK release date: January 13, 1978; US release date: January 24, 1978)

Label: Polar POLS 282

Notes

ABBA—The Album was ready just in time to be released in Scandinavia before Christmas, but in most other countries it was put back to the first couple of months of 1978, to be released in tandem with *ABBA—The Movie* and the "Take a Chance on Me" single.

NOTHING PROMISED,
NO REGRETS

Nothing Promised, No Regrets

January 1979 was an eventful month for ABBA. They had barely seen in the New Year before they had to board a plane and fly to New York City, where they were to take part in a UNICEF gala, kicking off the United Nations' Year of the Child. The gala, taking place at the General Assembly Hall in the United Nations building on January 9, had been instigated by The Bee Gees, their manager Robert Stigwood, and British television personality David Frost. As part of the concept, each of the participants would donate the royalties for the song they performed to UNICEF. While most of the artists put a time limit on their donation, ABBA signed away all rights to their song in perpetuity.

The tune in question was "Chiquitita," ABBA's new single, released a week after the gala. For UNICEF it turned out to be an especially lucrative deal as "Chiquitita" must rank as one of the group's most popular songs, almost up there with "Dancing Queen" and "Fernando." Its success was helped in no small part by a Spanish version recorded by ABBA in the spring of 1979, which became a massive hit in Latin America, some even claiming that it was the biggest hit in twenty-five years in that territory.

"Chiquitita" was indeed a major hit in most parts of the world, whether performed in English or Spanish. No doubt, the group were relieved after their most recent single, September 1978's Bee Gees-influenced nightlife celebration, "Summer Night City," hadn't quite delivered in the way they were used to. The ballad "Chiquitita" was more in line with the family-friendly "Fernando"-style songs that a large slice of their audience preferred.

The release of "Chiquitita" coincided with Björn and Agnetha's announcement that they were filing for divorce, made in the shape of an interview with a trusted journalist at Swedish newspaper *Expressen*. In the interview, the couple stressed that the split wasn't a matter of one of them having met someone else, it was just a matter of irreconcilable differences. The announcement was certainly a bombshell: After all, so much of the group's image had been constructed around the four members being two couples blissfully united in making glorious music. "That whole bit about an 'ideal image,' 'married bliss' and things like that has been created by the media," countered Agnetha. "At least it's not us ABBA members who have done that. We have been as we are and now there is a divorce—that's also a piece of our reality."

But how could ABBA possibly continue now that there had been a divorce within the group? Björn and Agnetha explained that they had discussed it and concluded that since ABBA wasn't the problem, there was no reason why they should give up on something they both enjoyed so much and that was working so well for them. If anything, they claimed, the split was beneficial for the working environment. "The tension that used to exist when we were working in the studio is gone," said Björn later in the year. "Today I can correct and criticise Agnetha without having to consider that she's my wife."

Nor did the publicity surrounding the divorce seem to harm ABBA in any way. On the contrary, their sixth album, *Voulez-Vous*—finally released on April 23, 1979—was a huge success. Thanks to "Chiquitita," the market of Latin America had now been opened up for them, making the album an even bigger seller. The same was true of Japan, where their success had been

PAGE 112 ABBA in Paris, France, 1978

OPPOSITE ABBA with John Denver (fourth, right), Olivia Newton-John (third, right), Andy Gibb (second, right), and Maurice Gibb (right), at the United Nations General Assembly, New York, during recording of a NBC TV special, *The Music for UNICEF concert*, January 1979

> **66 A lot of things happen on a purely emotional level onstage, in the studio and strictly privately, and it shines through on the records. 99**
>
> Agnetha

finding the solitude of the nighttime unbearable after a breakup, "were written during a period when I was feeling really depressed. I was down as hell." As he added some years later, "I'm sure it was something that hit me on a lonely night."

The bulk of the album was recorded at ABBA's brand-new Polar Music Studio in central Stockholm, which opened in May 1978. Björn, Benny, and engineer Michael B. Tretow had made a wish list of equipment, gadgets, and features they wanted in what was to be their dream studio, employing the services of top studio constructors. In a marked contrast to the often

comparatively limited for the first part of their career. Stig Anderson later remembered how they'd been told they couldn't possibly conquer Japan, since their music just wasn't right for that market. He proved the naysayers wrong after a campaign in 1978, involving a two-week trip to Japan in November, where ABBA met the media, recorded their own television special, and did all the promotion they could. As a result, the group established itself on the Japanese market, *Voulez-Vous* becoming their first No. 1 album. With the appropriate effort applied, it seemed no corner of the planet was immune to ABBA's charms.

The *Voulez-Vous* album was in some respects a step back for the group. Gone were the overtly ambitious complexities of *ABBA—The Album*, mini-musical and all, and back were the intense depictions of matters of the heart. Sometimes regarded as ABBA's disco album, because of the many dance-friendly tracks on it, it has to be said that few outright disco collections would include selections such as "Chiquitita" or the ballad "I Have a Dream," featuring a children's choir from the International School of Stockholm. But most of the tracks had an up-tempo and/or slightly funky feel to them—not least hit singles such as "Does Your Mother Know" and the title track, the backing track of which was recorded in Miami with bona fide American disco musicians—while the lyrics were all about nightclub flirting, desperate pleas for affection, or the price to be paid when love affairs go wrong.

Agnetha and Björn both admitted that their marital problems had colored the songs on the album. "I wonder if the record didn't turn out better because of it," said Agnetha. "A lot of things happen on a purely emotional level onstage, in the studio and strictly privately, and it shines through on the records." Shortly after the album's release, Björn stated that the lyrics for a track called "If It Wasn't for the Nights," about someone

BELOW AND OPPOSITE Frida (L) and Agnetha (R) onstage at Radio City Music Hall in New York City on October 2, 1979

dark, cramped spaces of the typical recording studio, the walls were decorated with panels of white clouds against a blue sky. The control room, usually something of an afterthought, was made to be spacious: After all, this was where Björn, Benny, and Michael would spend much of their time. Polar Music Studio was, quite simply, the realization of a long-held dream. "It's a joy working in that studio, because exactly everything is available there," enthused Benny. It also resolved a long-standing problem in acquiring enough studio time as they worked out their immaculately produced music: Now, as Björn commented, "we can virtually take as long as we want in the creative process—all day over an intro sequence, for instance."

With the exception of the "Voulez-Vous" backing track, all of ABBA's studio recordings would henceforth be made at Polar Music Studio. Being so modern and state-

of-the-art, it would also attract many other international artists over the decades. As early as the end of 1978, heavy rock superstars Led Zeppelin recorded their final studio album, *In Through the Out Door*, at Polar, while a year later Genesis used the facilities for their *Duke* album. The studio would live on until 2004.

In September 1979, ABBA embarked on their first tour of North America. The Americans had begged them to tour for several years since it was, at the time, the only way to break the United States. ABBA's lack of physical presence in America was probably what had kept them from conquering that market in the same extraordinary way they had Europe and Australia. It was a Catch-22 situation: If they wanted to become a hit act, they had to tour, but ABBA had argued that they didn't want to tour until they had become a hit act. By the time they started the North American tour,

they had notched up a number of Top Twenty hits, achieved a couple of platinum albums, and scored one chart-topping single in the shape of "Dancing Queen": a certain amount of credible success, then, if not at Australian Abbamania levels.

As it was, the tour was a rather limited outing of just a few weeks and not the ambitious trek across the vast continent that would have been required. Agnetha's determination that she should not be away from her children for more than a couple of weeks at a time was one factor, but, in truth, no one in the group was especially keen on touring. Björn and Benny, in particular, had done more than their share of traveling back and forth in Sweden in the 1960s and now got their kicks mainly from writing and recording music, not performing it onstage. For Frida it may have been just slightly different: Out of the four, she was the one who hadn't quite enjoyed the same adulation as the others before ABBA was formed, and it was only with the group that she truly found a way of functioning as a stage performer. "I think it's real fun being onstage," she reflected a few years prior to the tour of North America. "That's where I experience the happiest moments of my life. When I stand there, I'm completely exposed and open. I turn myself inside out and have nothing against revealing myself. I feel secure because I enjoy what I'm doing."

The tour kicked off with a show in Edmonton, Alberta, Canada on September 13 and progressed from there to other Canadian cities before continuing to the United States and then going back to Canada, concluding in Toronto on October 7. The stage presentation was the result of a collaboration between ABBA art director Rune Söderqvist and their trusted costume designer, Owe Sandström. The pair decided on an icy color scheme that played off ABBA's origins in the

LEFT ABBA live onstage in 1979 wearing glacier-inspired stage costumes designed by Owe Sandström

northernmost part of Europe, with different shades of purple, blue, and white. Söderqvist designed a stage construction based on icebergs, while Agnetha and Frida were dressed in Sandström's spandex outfits, featuring diagonal stripes inspired by glacier rivers. Similarly, Björn wore a body-hugging purple costume, with Benny more loosely dressed in blue and white.

Like most acts on tour, ABBA elected to showcase songs from their most recent album. All the singles from *Voulez-Vous* were performed, along with a couple of LP tracks, the group otherwise working their way through their by now impressive catalog of hits and familiar album tracks from 1975 onwards, the most notable exception perhaps being "Mamma Mia," one of their very biggest. At first they didn't even perform "Waterloo," probably feeling that it represented a stage of their career they had left behind them, but a few shows into the tour it was added to the show, presented as a "golden oldie."

Again, critics and audiences didn't always have the same experience when confronted with ABBA live in concert. While some music journalists came to the shows with their rock glasses on—knowing full well

that they were not going to get Led Zeppelin or The Ramones, but somehow still wishing they were—the reception from those who had paid for their tickets was decidedly more positive. At every show during the tour, a children's choir from whichever city they were in was brought onstage to sing along during "I Have a Dream"—as indeed a choir had done on the original record—and such family-friendly features would have been completely alien to your average 1970s rock critics. "Watching Abba live is like watching TV—there is some minimal illusion of action taking place but it's all very distant and compact," wrote critic Jim Farber of the group's New York show. All the while, ABBA's fans seemed to lap up every second.

For Agnetha, the 1979 tour was a decidedly mixed experience. On the one hand, she couldn't help being affected by the electric excitement of being onstage, with the love of an adoring audience flowing toward her. But on the other, she was not in an especially good place as a human being when the tour kicked off, and she just didn't want to be away from her children. "I don't know how I managed," she told author

Brita Åhman many years later. "The others were in a different phase and held up better. They didn't have children at home who had just gone through their parents' divorce. I was the one who had to live with a constant bad conscience. No one understood how painful it was. It's still difficult to talk about it." Agnetha and Björn's six-year-old daughter, Linda, came out to visit when ABBA were based in California, even making her stage debut during ABBA's Las Vegas show, and the chance to spend time with her daughter provided some comfort for Agnetha.

But just as the tour was reaching its end, disaster struck. On Wednesday, October 3, ABBA flew out of New York on a chartered private jet, their destination being Boston and their show that night. However, they soon encountered exceptionally bad weather, which meant they were unable to land at the designated airport. Everyone on board worried that they would

OPPOSITE Agnetha swims with daughter Linda during a break in ABBA's North American tour, September 1979
BELOW Björn speaks to the press while he relaxes poolside, September 1979

be forced to cancel that evening's concert, and the pilot didn't quite know what to do. For Agnetha, already suffering from a fear of flying, the flight turned into her worst nightmare. When the pilot realized he was running out of fuel, he and his co-pilot decided to make an emergency landing. But this turned out to be something of a challenge. "Our lives were in mortal danger—that's how it felt for me—with flashes on the wings and without being able to see anything," Agnetha recalled. "Everything was just black, and the plane was shaking something horribly. I prayed to God that I wouldn't die."

As the plane finally landed safely, although she felt unsteady Agnetha was able to go through with the Boston show. But after the concert, the nightmarish experience caught up with her. As the entourage arrived in Washington the following day, Agnetha became physically ill and barricaded herself in her room, refusing to come out. There was nothing else to do than to cancel the Washington show, although the remaining dates on the itinerary were seen through. The horrendous experience on the plane did nothing to improve Agnetha's attitude toward touring.

RIGHT Björn and Agnetha (top) and Björn and Frida (bottom) onstage at Wembley Arena, London, November 9, 1979

OPPOSITE Japan welcomes ABBA, March 1980

After about ten days in Stockholm, ABBA embarked on the second leg of their tour, taking in Europe this time and encompassing Sweden, Denmark, France, the Netherlands, West Germany, Switzerland, Austria, Belgium, England, Scotland, and Ireland, the last show taking place in Dublin on November 15, Frida's thirty-fourth birthday. In a marked contrast to their 1977 London shows, this time there was no worry that they might not sell out whatever venues they booked in the British capital, seeing through six consecutive sell-out shows at Wembley Arena. Although ABBA were under siege from fans wherever they went, the European outing went off without any of the drama that marked the North American tour, all shows except the Paris concert being sold out, confirming their superstar status.

In conjunction with the tour, a brand-new single was released. "Gimme! Gimme! Gimme! (A Man after Midnight)" extended the dance-friendly beats from the *Voulez-Vous* album, casting lead singer Agnetha in the role of a desperate woman, yearning for some nighttime company. The single was a convincing hit in most places—their biggest success that year with the

exception of "Chiquitita"—and the only new track on ABBA's second album of the year, *Greatest Hits Vol. 2*. Coming just a few years after the previous *Greatest Hits* collection, its release could have seemed a bit premature if it had been by any act other than ABBA. As it was, each of the fourteen tracks on the album had been a Top Five hit in at least one country, the exception being "I Wonder (Departure)," culled from *ABBA—The Album* and only issued on a single as an alternate live version on the B-side of "The Name of the Game." Needless to say, this hits collection was immensely successful, selling more than one million copies in the UK before the end of the year.

The end of the European part of the tour was followed by almost four months away from the concert stage, before the third and final leg of the tour began in Japan at Tokyo's famous Budokan arena on March 12, 1980. By now, ABBA had become so huge in Japan that the hysteria was on the same level as everywhere else. Landing at Narita Airport they were met by some one hundred photographers who did their best to break through the line of two hundred policemen who tried to guard the group. At the hotel, they were hardly

66 **Our songs were so tightly constructed and on stage we were trying to recreate the sound we had created in the studio, so we were really restricted.** 99

Björn

able to venture outside their rooms. "We had two floors to ourselves, which had been shut off," recalled tour producer Thomas Johansson. "At one point Agnetha and my wife tried to leave their rooms to get something to eat, but that turned out to be impossible. Then they wanted to visit the sauna and spa area in the hotel, but that was also impossible. In the end that entire section had to be shut off, just so that they could make their way there."

Agnetha, knowing that Linda would start school in the autumn of 1980, and being adamant that she should be there to support her daughter, wanted to cut down severely on ABBA's traveling in the future. As for concert tours, perhaps with the exception of Frida, no one in the group was especially keen on it anyway and they were only happy to get out of it. "I did still get a buzz from performing at the beginning of each tour with ABBA," Björn told author Philip Dodd several decades later, "but it wore off quite quickly and then it became tedious, not so much from the constant moving on tour, although that is naturally difficult, but more because as a group we always had to do the same thing at the same time. . . . Our songs were so tightly constructed and on stage we were trying to recreate the sound we had created in the studio, so we were really restricted."

The recording studio was the group's natural home, and working there, spending hours, days, and weeks perfecting each and every song, was the purpose of their existence in the first place. ABBA's show at the Budokan on March 27, 1980 turned out to be their last concert in front of a paying audience.

LEFT ABBA, Tokyo, Japan, March 1980
OVERLEAF ABBA perform in front of 10,000 fans in Tokyo, Japan on March 13, 1980

VOULEZ-VOUS

SIDE ONE

As Good as New
Voulez-Vous
I Have a Dream
Angeleyes
The King Has Lost His Crown

SIDE TWO

Does Your Mother Know
If It Wasn't for the Nights
Chiquitita
Lovers (Live a Little Longer)
Kisses of Fire

Recorded: Marcus Music, Glenstudio, Polar Music Studio, Stockholm, Sweden, and Criteria Studios, Miami, Florida, United States

Produced and arranged by: Benny Andersson and Björn Ulvaeus

Engineered by: Michael B. Tretow

Personnel:
Agnetha Fältskog: vocals
Anni-Frid Lyngstad: vocals
Björn Ulvaeus: vocals, guitar, banjo
Benny Andersson: vocals, keyboards
Paul Harris: piano
Janne Schaffer, Lasse Wellander, Ish Ledesma, George Terry: guitar
Rutger Gunnarsson: bass, string arrangements
Arnold Paseiro, Mike Watson: bass
Ola Brunkert, Joe Galdo, Rolf Alex: drums
Malando Gassama: percussion
Lars O. Carlsson, Halldor Pálsson, Johan Stengård, Kajtek Wojciechowski: saxophones
Nils Landgren: trombone
Jan Risberg: oboe
Anders Eljas: string and horn arrangements
International School of Stockholm Choir, directed by Kerstin Feist: vocals

Cover art:
Rune Söderqvist: layout
Ola Lager: photography

Released: April 23, 1979 (UK release date: May 4, 1979; US release date: June 13, 1979)

Label: Polar POLS 292

Notes
ABBA's 1978 single "Summer Night City," recorded during sessions for *Voulez-Vous*, originally featured a piano/strings/vocals introduction, which was edited from the track for single release. The full-length version was meant to be featured on *Voulez-Vous* but was ultimately left off, remaining unreleased until its inclusion on the 1994 CD box set *Thank You for the Music*.

GREATEST HITS VOL. 2

ABBA® Greatest Hits Vol.2

SIDE ONE

Gimme! Gimme! Gimme!
  (A Man after Midnight)
Knowing Me, Knowing You
Take a Chance on Me
Money, Money, Money
Rock Me
Eagle
Angeleyes

SIDE TWO

Dancing Queen
Does Your Mother Know
Chiquitita
Summer Night City
I Wonder (Departure)
The Name of the Game
Thank You for the Music

Cover art:
Rune Söderqvist: layout
Ola Lager: photography

Released: October 29, 1979 (UK release date: October 26, 1979; US release date: November 1979)

Label: Polar POLS 312

Notes

While most of the selections on this album were well-known international hit singles, "Rock Me" was a bit of an anomaly. Originally featured on the B-side of the chart-topping "I Do, I Do, I Do, I Do, I Do" single in Australia, it was flipped over at the height of Abbamania, causing the single to climb up the charts all over again, peaking at an impressive No. 4.

SHINING LIKE
THE SUN

Shining Like The Sun

In between the end of ABBA's tour of Europe in November 1979 and the Japanese trek in March 1980 it wasn't exactly as if the members sat around twiddling their thumbs. The extraordinary boost on the Latin American market, achieved just through the recording of "Chiquitita" in Spanish, suggested that this should be further pursued. In August 1979, just prior to the tour of North America, ABBA added Spanish vocals to "I Have a Dream," entitled "Estoy soñando," and released it as a single. When this also became a sizeable hit, the next logical step was to record an entire album in Spanish.

The new lyrics were written by RCA Argentina employee Buddy McCluskey in collaboration with his wife Mary. In January 1980, engineer Michael B. Tretow convened with Agnetha and Frida in his home studio to add new vocals to the existing backing tracks. They also had help from Sweden-based Argentine journalist and broadcaster Ana Martinez del Valle, who would recall being a little doubtful that two Scandinavian singers would be able to convince as Spanish-language performers. But once they stood in front of the microphones, her doubts vanished. "What happened was *magia*—magic! It was such a change from being with them outside the studio, going through the lyrics and discussing them, and then them going into the studio and singing with such intensity that they could have been two Latinas. I thought it was extraordinary."

The album, entitled *Gracias por la música* ("Thank You for the Music" in Spanish), was hugely successful. Three months after release, it had already been certified 4 x Platinum in Argentina, also selling well in many other Latin American countries, going Platinum and reaching No. 2 on the charts in Spain, and even entering the charts in ABBA-crazy Japan. *Gracias por la música* was also released as a mid-price album in most other markets, albeit not promoted heavily and thus not making much of a mark. All in all, though, the Spanish-language adventure had proved worthwhile, even though the male half of the band kept the project at arm's length: Benny once admitted that he had "never ever listened to the Spanish album, except to okay it when it was finished."

While Agnetha and Frida were working on *Gracias por la música*, Björn and Benny began writing songs for the next proper ABBA album. A year earlier, during the troublesome *Voulez-Vous* sessions, they had attempted to get fresh stimulation for their songwriting by traveling to the Bahamas, borrowing a house owned by Atlantic Records, the group's American record company. What they were after in particular were fresh impulses from contemporary music. At this time, Sweden didn't have any commercial radio and Sveriges Radio—the equivalent of BBC Radio in the UK—didn't exactly shower the listeners with contemporary pop music. Björn and Benny could of course afford to buy whatever records they were interested in, but radio had the advantage of offering surprises: As you turned the dial on American radio, you would be exposed to music that you didn't even know existed, and in a variety of different genres. "We wrote, listened to the radio, and wrote some more," recalled Björn.

The trip was successful: Not only did they write the title tune of *Voulez-Vous* in the Bahamas, but fired up by the excitement they booked time at Criteria Studios in Miami and recorded its backing track there. After they returned home, in early February 1979, half of the tracks on the album were completed in just a couple

PAGE 132 Agnetha and Frida during the video and album cover shoot for the *Super Trouper* album, October 1980
OPPOSITE In Sweden, October 1980

of months, whereas it had taken them nine months to come up with the first half.

Small wonder, then, that they were eager to repeat the experiment in January 1980. This time, however, they went to another Caribbean location, namely Barbados. Benny remembered a house there from two years earlier, when he and Frida had been vacationing on the island. They hadn't stayed there themselves, but another power couple from a successful 1970s band had. Paul and Linda McCartney of Wings invited Benny and Frida to come over for drinks one night, and the ex-Beatle's abode made quite an impression on Benny. "It was a really nice house," he recalled. "It was like a hotel where you were the only guest. There was staff who cooked and cleaned for you." As a contrast to the chilly Swedish winter of January 1980, Benny figured it might be inspirational. "I thought, 'We should go there to break the stalemate and concentrate on writing songs for a week or so, in a nice environment.'"

In Barbados, Benny and Björn met up with comedian John Cleese and his daughter, having dinner with them, a big thrill for the two Swedish Monty Python fans. During the dinner, Björn and Benny suggested that maybe Cleese would like to write the book for a musical they were planning, constructed around a New Year's Eve. Cleese politely declined, but the initial idea survived in the shape of the reflective Agnetha-sung ballad "Happy New Year," subsequently recorded for ABBA's forthcoming album.

This tune and at least one other were written in Barbados before Björn and Benny got homesick and flew home to Sweden. Nevertheless, the trip had clearly got their creative juices flowing, for between the start of the first period of sessions for the new album, on February 4, 1980, and its end in little over a week later, on February 12, no less than five backing tracks had been completed—an extraordinary contrast to the slow uphill struggle of *Voulez-Vous*. Album sessions were interrupted by tour rehearsals and then the Japanese trek, concluding at the end of March. By April 9, the group were back at Polar Music Studio to start recording vocals for the new songs.

While things seemed to be running smoothly for ABBA as a musical entity, there was plenty of other drama going on behind the scenes, mainly concerning their business interests. Following the death of Polar

Music co-founder Bengt Bernhag in 1971, Stig had become the sole proprietor of the record company. Then, in April 1975, Björn and Benny acquired 50 percent of Polar through their own company Harlequin. A couple of years later, Agnetha and Frida in turn became equal part-owners of Harlequin, meaning that the four members each owned 12.5 percent of Polar Music, while Stig owned 50 percent. Around the same time, the company was restructured and was henceforth known formally as Polar Music International.

As a consequence of ABBA's extraordinary success, the money was flowing in to Polar Music. In percentage terms, it was reported, Polar's profits were even larger than Volvo's. These reports were misunderstood to mean that they actually earned more money than the car manufacturer—of course, in terms of dollars and cents there was no way they could compete with an industry giant such as Volvo. Nevertheless, Polar profits were large, which was certainly a nice turn of events, but also created a problem: What were they to do with their newfound wealth?

For as long as anyone can remember, taxes have been high in Sweden, and back in the 1970s high earners such as Stig and ABBA would have to pay a whopping 85 percent tax if they declared the capital as income. The answer, of course, was to invest their profits. Up to 1977, Stig's wife, Gudrun, had been mainly responsible for Polar's financial affairs, although she was more or less self-taught. The company had invested in real estate, but as Polar's profits increased they realized they needed to diversify and acquire professional help with the investments. "I don't know how to do that," commented Gudrun. "I don't have the education—I'm a weaving teacher."

Another problem related to ABBA and Polar's finances was the need to find a way to get paid properly for the group's extraordinary record sales in the Eastern Bloc, where regulations stipulated that only a limited amount of money was allowed out of those countries, effectively locking in payments for imported goods and services. Someone came up with the clever idea that bartering schemes might be the way to go, the thinking being that in lieu of being paid in cash, companies owned by Polar could exchange record royalties for goods that would

be imported from the Eastern Bloc, sold in Sweden and elsewhere, and then turned into cash. For a few years several such schemes were entered into, but not many of them turned out particularly well. Perhaps the biggest disaster occurred in 1980, when Polar formed a company called Pol Oil and bought 55,000 tons of crude oil on the spot market in Rotterdam, the intention being that it should be sold immediately and at a higher price, common practice in the oil business. But things didn't turn out as planned: The oil remained unsold and Pol Oil was ultimately forced to sell it at a price way below the purchase price, causing a loss of a whopping thirty million kronor (£3.3 million at the time), directly affecting the personal finances of ABBA and their manager. By June 1980, Pol Oil had closed down.

OPPOSITE Agnetha and Björn on the set of the "Happy New Year" video shoot, October 1980

RIGHT ABBA's Manager Stig Anderson and his wife Gudrun pictured at the Eurovision Song Contest, Dublin, Ireland, April 1981

Of course, not all investments Polar Music engaged in were disastrous: On the contrary, many of them were in fact quite successful. For example, at one point they bought a major Swedish bicycle manufacturer called Monark, simply for the purpose of using it in a complex tax avoidance set-up, but when they sold the company, it was in much better shape than when they acquired it. Nevertheless, over the next couple of years, the business schemes and complex tax avoidance strategies would become ever-more intricate, somehow taking on a life of their own and worming their way into the public ABBA narrative. The business aspects were something the media loved to write about and comment on, which was not particularly good for ABBA's public image, as such writings fueled the perception that they "were only in it for the money."

Ironically, around the time of the Pol Oil disaster, ABBA were on one of their most impressive creative streaks, with all four members being at the top of their game. In late May 1980, Björn and Benny traveled out to their beloved songwriting cabin on Viggsö to write more songs for the new album. When they returned to Stockholm and Polar Music Studios on June 2, they had on their hands two absolute highlights, not only on the album but in the entire ABBA canon. The first to be attempted was a song adorned with the working title "The Story of My Life," which they had high hopes for. A jaunty, four-on-the-floor backing track, punctuated with handclaps, was committed to tape. But listening to a rough mix in the car on their way home, the two songwriters felt it sounded okay but not quite as great as it should. "It was an important song," recalled Björn, "and we wanted to make sure that we didn't 'lose' it."

Four days later, they made a new attempt. In between the first backing track and this new recording session, Benny had come up with some descending piano lines, which would be heard in the song's intro and then regularly throughout the recording. Also, instead of the metrical backing, the new version had a looser, more ebb-and-flow feel. With this new arrangement the songwriters felt they were moving just slightly into French chanson territory, causing Björn to record demo vocals consisting of random French phrases. Since the group liked to have at least one Björn-led song on each album, there was a suggestion that perhaps he should helm this one. Fortunately, that thought didn't last very long and the song was instead given to Agnetha.

Björn took a tape of the new backing track home and set about writing the lyrics. Listening to the tape over and over, he opened a bottle of whisky and had "a couple of big snifters," as he would recall. In this slightly tipsy state, the words came to him almost immediately, taking less than an hour from idea to completed lyrics. "That never works, writing when you're drunk," he remembered, "you think it's wonderful but it looks terrible the next day, but that one worked." When he laid down pen and paper, the song had been given the title "The Winner Takes It All."

> **"That never works, writing when you're drunk, you think it's wonderful but it looks terrible the next day, but that one worked."**
>
> Björn

When Agnetha came to the studio to record the vocals, Björn showed her the lyrics; as she read them, he would later remember, "a tear or two welled up in her eyes." Was it because the words were a literal depiction of what had happened to Björn and Agnetha in their marriage? The two divorcees would both argue no. Their marital split hadn't been a matter of winners or losers, but was simply the sad but inevitable and mutual conclusion of a relationship that had lost its spark.

However, there was an emotional truth in the narrative: Lyricist Björn later admitted that "the theme of a divorce or going separate ways was on my mind—the anguish surrounding that situation." And from singer Agnetha's perspective, maybe some lines resonated more strongly than others. On New Year's Eve 1978, just a week after Agnetha left their home on Christmas Day, Björn had struck up a relationship with a woman named Lena Källersjö at a party hosted by Benny and Frida. Although Agnetha hadn't been jilted, the decision to end the marriage being as much hers as Björn's, maybe she couldn't resist wondering if Lena kissed Björn "like I used to kiss you," as the lyrics had it.

Even beyond any such real-life considerations, "The Winner Takes It All" was to the point and hard-hitting about the emotional consequences of ending a relationship. Agnetha's vocal performance was her best-ever, and the simplicity of the song—only two melody lines are repeated throughout the course of it—combined with the subtle changes in the arrangement and the mood-shifts in the lyrics, made it a masterclass in how to write and produce a pop song. "I listen to it when my self-esteem is low," Agnetha would point out many years later. "I can pat myself on the back, 'you did well there.'" When released as a single in July 1980, "The Winner Takes It All" returned ABBA to the UK No. 1 spot for the first time in more than two years, and became the group's final Top Ten hit in the US. Today, the song is widely regarded as one of ABBA's best works.

The second song brought to the studio around this time was never released as a single A-side and so never got the chance to become a worldwide hit, but it was no less compelling. "Our Last Summer," a mid-tempo number recorded in between the two versions of "The Winner Takes It All," featured a lead vocal performance by Frida that was just as masterful and emotionally charged as Agnetha's. Similarly, the lyrics had a connection to something that Björn himself had experienced. In the 1960s, when he was in his teens, he visited a girl from his hometown who was working as an au pair in Paris. "We had not been romantically involved in Sweden," he told author Philip Dodd, "but Paris tends to have that effect on people, and so it was with the two of us. She certainly took me to see the Quartier Latin, the Champs-Élysées and the Eiffel Tower, but to be honest I don't really remember much of Paris. I mostly remember her!" When writing the tune, the songwriters had noticed a strong touch of nostalgia inherent in it. This triggered Björn's associations with his romantic Paris visit, resulting in, as he phrased it, a "melancholy memory of 'the last summer of innocence.'"

Frida was assigned the lead vocal duties, somehow managing to make Björn's story her own. Reflective, where Agnetha was melodramatic in "The Winner Takes It All," Frida expressed both the joy of the romance she was experiencing in Paris and the wistful regret that it was all now in the past and impossible to recapture. One poignant moment in the second verse captures this duality perfectly. On the lines, "I was so happy we had met / it was the age of no regret / oh yes," Frida sounds just slightly strained on the "oh yes," as if she's about to burst into tears, suggesting that she was aware, even when the romance was ongoing, that there would indeed be plenty of regret ahead. In other words, in the affirmative "oh yes," an "oh no" is already embedded.

"The Winner Takes It All" and "Our Last Summer" were not only two examples of the group's exemplary craftsmanship, but they also highlighted the different strengths of the two singers. Ironically, Frida has expressed how much she loves "The Winner Takes It All" and that she would have loved to be the lead singer on it, while "Our Last Summer" is one of Agnetha's standout ABBA favorites, suggesting that she maybe envied Frida for being its chosen vocalist.

By late September 1980, ABBA's new, as yet untitled album was more or less ready for release, and it was high time that a sleeve was put together. Agnetha, Björn, Benny, and Frida were now superstars who could afford to be indulgent if they wanted to, and so, together with their trusted album designer, Rune Söderqvist, they worked out their most ambitious sleeve concept yet. The exact thought process is lost to time, but they somehow arrived at the idea that they should shoot the album cover at London's Piccadilly Circus, with ABBA surrounded by a real circus troupe. Söderqvist flew to London to make all the necessary arrangements, but soon realized that they had to abandon the idea: It transpired that local regulations prohibited the wearing of "funny costumes" in the West End, to prevent publicity stunts from the many theaters and other entertainment venues in the area. Instead, a Stockholm film studio was hired, and a large number of friends and acquaintances were gathered, together with bona fide circus performers, to create a slightly surreal spectacle and atmosphere.

It was in this environment that they finally found the title for the album. The many spotlights in the studio got Björn and Benny thinking about the type of gigantic spotlights used at stadium shows, trademarked as Super Troupers. But not only was *Super Trouper* a good name for the album, but the phrase also happened to fit perfectly for the chorus of a brand-new song they had recorded at Polar Music Studios earlier on the day of the sleeve shoot. The Frida-led "Super Trouper" became the group's new single—their ninth and final UK No. 1—issued in tandem with the album.

For Björn, Benny, and engineer Michael B. Tretow, *Super Trouper* is ABBA's most satisfactory album. It's not hard to understand why: Björn and Benny were striving toward the overtly sophisticated and adult, as well as for musical perfection, with everything tightly under control and most of the rough spots meticulously ironed out. Benny's sophisticated Yamaha GX-1 synthesizer, acquired during the previous year's *Voulez-Vous* sessions, dominated the soundscape on *Super Trouper*, and the only track to feature real live strings was "The Winner Takes It All," the string sounds on "Happy New Year," for example, being generated by the GX-1.

For those who enjoyed ABBA's rough spots, maybe the album was a little too mature and over-polished. Except for "The Winner Takes It All" and the magnificent electro-disco of "Lay All Your Love on Me," there was little of the unrelenting desperation that had put a mark on the *Voulez-Vous* album. "On and On and On," about whimsical high-society flirting,

aspired to be a rocker, but with Benny's GX-1 trying but not quite succeeding in sounding like electric guitars, the recording perhaps became a little too smooth; Benny himself would later regret that there weren't more electric guitars on the track.

Most record-buyers seemed to want ABBA exactly this way, though, as the album sold in the millions all over the world, attracting more than one million advance orders in the UK alone and going to No. 1 in nine countries. By the looks of it, ABBA seemed unstoppable and were just getting bigger and bigger.

OPPOSITE Recording "Our Last Summer" in June 1980
BELOW Björn and Benny with Rune Söderqvist (R)
OVERLEAF At the album sleeve shoot for *Super Trouper*, 1980

GRACIAS POR LA MUSICA

SIDE ONE

Gracias por la música
– Thank You for the Music –
Reina danzante
– Dancing Queen –
Al andar
– Move On –
¡Dame! ¡Dame! ¡Dame!
– Gimme! Gimme! Gimme!
   (A Man after Midnight) –
Fernando

SIDE TWO

Estoy soñando
– I Have a Dream –
Mamma mía
Hasta mañana
Conociéndome, conociéndote
– Knowing Me, Knowing You –
Chiquitita

Cover art:
Rune Söderqvist, Lasse Liljendahl: layout
Heinz Angemayr: photography

Released: June 23, 1980 (UK release date: July 18, 1980; US release date: circa June 1980)

Label: SEPTIMA SRLM 1

Notes

The success of ABBA's Spanish-language recordings led to the inclusion of two Spanish-language versions of songs on their final two studio albums, in Spanish and Latin American markets. *Super Trouper* features Spanish versions of "Andante, Andante" and "Happy New Year" ("Felicidad"), while *The Visitors* includes "No hay a quien culpar" ("When All Is Said and Done") and "Se me está escapando" ("Slipping through My Fingers"). All of ABBA's Spanish-language tracks were eventually collected on the 1999 version of the CD compilation *ABBA Oro*, which also featured a Spanish version of "Ring Ring," recorded in 1973 but not released at the time.

SUPER TROUPER

SIDE ONE

Super Trouper
The Winner Takes It All
On and On and On
Andante, Andante
Me and I

SIDE TWO

Happy New Year
Our Last Summer
The Piper
Lay All Your Love on Me
The Way Old Friends Do

Recorded: Polar Music Studio, Stockholm, Sweden, and Wembley Arena, London, England

Produced and arranged by: Benny Andersson and Björn Ulvaeus

Engineered by: Michael B. Tretow

Personnel:
Agnetha Fältskog: vocals
Anni-Frid Lyngstad: vocals
Björn Ulvaeus: vocals, guitar
Benny Andersson: vocals, keyboards
Janne Schaffer, Lasse Wellander: guitar
Rutger Gunnarsson: bass, string arrangements
Mike Watson: bass
Ola Brunkert, Per Lindvall: drums
Åke Sundqvist: percussion
Lars O. Carlsson, Kajtek Wojciechowski: saxophones
Janne Kling: saxophone, flute

Cover art:
Rune Söderqvist: layout
Lars Larsson: photography

Released: November 3, 1980 (UK release date: November 21, 1980; US release date: November 21, 1980)

Label: Polar POLS 322

Notes
A song called "Put On Your White Sombrero" was left off the album and not released until the 1994 box set *Thank You for the Music*. In the twenty-first century, Benny Andersson has grown so fond of the song that he performs it live with his Benny Anderssons orkester.

FEELING THE
AUTUMN CHILL

Feeling The Autumn Chill

The making of the *Super Trouper* album had been a comparatively smooth ride. At least it looked that way from the outside, as song after song kept pouring out of Björn and Benny in the course of 1980. But the months immediately following its release were anything but quiet.

Promotional trips to West Germany and the UK had been booked for November, but they were swiftly cancelled when the group received a kidnap threat, variously reported as concerning an unspecified ABBA member or Björn and Agnetha's daughter, Linda. The group was advised by the police to stay in Stockholm, and so huge were ABBA at this time that the producers of the West German television program *Show Express*, determined to have ABBA on their show, simply brought their props to a studio in Stockholm, broadcasting the appearance via link-up. The kidnap threat turned out to be a hoax, although the fact that it had come at all certainly was enough to cause quite a bit of worry within the group. "When that sort of thing becomes a reality it's awful," Björn reflected some years later. "Suddenly it dawns on you that there might be some crazy bastard out there."

On a happier note, in January 1981, Björn and Lena Källersjö were married in a simple ceremony. The low-key affair was the opposite of the chaos that surrounded Björn and Agnetha's ceremony ten years earlier. More pertinently, in terms of ABBA's public image, the marriage underlined the fact that Agnetha and Björn really weren't a couple anymore, ending all possible speculation that they might get back together again. And four decades later, Björn and Lena remain happily married.

PAGE 148 Frida and Benny, Stockholm, Sweden, October 17, 1979
OPPOSITE Braving the pouring rain in London, UK, in 1974

> ## "It was a terribly frustrating time. We both wanted something else and yet, as members of the group, we had to present a happy, united front to the public."
>
> Frida

But only weeks after their wedding, the world was shocked to learn that the remaining marriage within ABBA had collapsed: In an announcement on February 12, 1981, Benny and Frida let the world know that they were going to divorce. It was an ironic turn of events, as the Ulvaeus–Fältskog marriage collapse back in 1978 occurred at the same time as Benny and Frida decided to tie the knot.

The marriage had been moving toward its inevitable end for quite some time. Where they had once wanted to hold the relationship together, however stormy it had been at times, lately things had changed. "It was a terribly frustrating time," recalled Frida. "We both wanted something else and yet, as members of the group, we had to present a happy, united front to the public." Looking back on this period, she would reflect on how ABBA had engulfed their entire lives so that it became almost impossible to say where their relationship as husband and wife ended and the group started. The ABBA machinery provided something to hold on to and a reason to stay together: Later, Benny would even suggest that if it hadn't been for the group, both marriages within ABBA would have ended much earlier. Like Björn and Agnetha, he and Frida had sought help from a marriage counselor, but nothing seemed to help.

The way out was finally provided by the arrival of another woman in Benny's life. At a party in September 1980, Benny was seated next to a lady by the name of Mona Nörklit. She was hardly a stranger to him for she was the sister of Lillebil Ankarcrona: Lillebil was the partner of album designer Rune Söderqvist, and the inventor of the *Arrival* album title; the Söderqvist–Ankarcrona couple were very close to Benny and Frida. But at this party, Benny began viewing Mona in a completely different light. "It took me 15 minutes to realise that I was sitting next to a woman who would change my life," he recalled. "I don't know how it happened. It just hit me. It was one of those things in life that you can't resist. We talked non-stop for eight hours, but I have no idea about what!"

He wasn't about to start an affair with Mona behind Frida's back, and so a difficult conversation had to take place. Despite Frida's dissatisfaction with the marriage, she had maybe assumed that they could patch things up, but now any such hopes were shattered, as Benny moved out of their stately home into an apartment in central Stockholm. "When you realise that he's walking out the door for the last time, then it hurts," Frida told a reporter some time later. "Then you get scared: will I be able to deal with my life? There are so many things that you have to handle. Everything from mundane matters to the most intimate physical and psychological needs."

Where Björn and Agnetha had announced their split in the shape of a fairly extensive interview, Frida and Benny only issued a rather terse statement. "We're aware that there will be a lot of speculation in the media but we'll have to take that," they declared. "Our private life is our own business and no-one else has anything to do with that. This step doesn't affect ABBA's continued collaboration in any way, but is of a strictly private nature. We don't wish to make any further comments."

The end of the marriage may not have had an immediate effect on the group as an entity, but it certainly made its mark on one of the first songs to be recorded for ABBA's next album, in March 1981. Among the songs was a tune entitled "When All Is Said and Done," the lyrics for which were directly triggered by Benny and Frida's marital split. "It was so sad, even sadder in a way than my own divorce not too long before," Björn related many years later. "Maybe because I was watching it from the outside. And when the tune of 'When All Is Said and Done' was finished and ready to be lyricized I wanted to write something

OPPOSITE Appearing live via satellite from Stockholm, Sweden on the West German TV program *Show Express*, 1980

BELOW ABBA in Bournemouth, UK, September 1981

about them and what they went through. Something that gave my friends credit for courage and dignity."

Naturally, Frida was the designated lead singer of "When All Is Said and Done," and she certainly appreciated Björn's efforts. "All my sadness was captured in that song," she once admitted. Elaborated Björn, "It was something that had happened to people close to me, something that triggered the lyrics. It was the finality of it all: 'when all is said and done.' The lyrics looked at a period in time, an era, and put a full stop to it. Because that's really what they did. Neither for them, nor for me and Agnetha, was there ever a question of perhaps getting back together again—this was the end." Frida's vocal performance, delivered with passion and conviction, is nothing short of astonishing, turning "When All Is Said and Done" into a powerful companion to the previous year's "The Winner Takes It All," Agnetha's breakup tour de force.

LEFT Frida during the video shoot for "When All Is Said and Done", August 1981

As soon as Frida and Benny's divorce became final, in November 1981, Benny married Mona, who by that time was already heavily pregnant. Similarly, Björn and Lena were expecting their first child around the same time, so the male half of ABBA was in good shape in terms of romance and moving on with their lives. It was more difficult for the two women. Since her divorce announcement in 1979, Agnetha had gone through two short-lived relationships: first with elite ice-hockey player Lars-Erik Ericsson and then with Dick Håkansson, the director of a women's clothes manufacturer. But before the end of 1980, she was a single woman again.

ABBA's first studio recording of 1981 was a tribute to their manager, Stig Anderson, for his fiftieth birthday, on January 25. Entitled "Hovas vittne" ("Hova's Witness,"

a pun on Hova, the small town in Sweden where Stig grew up), the catchy song featured a tongue-in-cheek list of Stig's characteristics and personal quirks, such as his habit of starting the vacuum cleaner when he wanted party guests to leave his house. At his birthday party, a video clip featuring ABBA performing the song dressed in their "Waterloo" costumes was shown. Stig was also gifted the publishing contract for the song on the condition that it would never be recorded with any other lyrics than the original words; Stig, always a music publisher first and foremost, couldn't resist commenting later that it was a pity that such a good song couldn't be put to better use. Indeed, ABBA's recording has never been officially released, only distributed as a limited edition 12-inch single—two hundred copies were made—to party guests.

In mid-March, ABBA were back in the studio, kicking

off sessions for their eighth studio album. "When All Is Said and Done" was among those first tracks, along with the ballad "Slipping through My Fingers," which carried strong personal resonance for Björn himself. When the lyrics were written, his and Agnetha's daughter, Linda, had been in school for about six months (Swedish children start school at age seven), causing her father to reflect on where all the time had gone. He was sitting in Agnetha's kitchen when he was overcome with emotion. "I was watching Linda going away to school, turning around and waving, and I thought, 'Now she has taken that step, she's going away—what have I missed out on through all these years?', which is a feeling I think every parent has." It was self-evident that Linda's mother would be the lead singer, later commenting that the lyrics felt very "true."

Notably, the sessions for the new album had begun with two of ABBA's most personal songs, and Björn's increasing sense of liberation as a lyricist would put its mark on the album. He recalled penning the words for these two songs in particular, on a skiing holiday with his wife Lena. "I remember that it was such a joy doing that because I felt, 'I can say exactly whatever I want here.' Suddenly I was inserting a bit of personal stuff in the lyrics."

"Slipping through My Fingers" was one of two new songs (the other being the Björn-led nudge-nudge number "Two for the Price of One") performed as ABBA took a break from album sessions toward the end of April to record a television special entitled *Dick Cavett Meets ABBA*. The famous American talk show host had been brought over to Sweden to interview the group in what purported to be a light-hearted conversation, which was then followed by a live concert. The problem was that Cavett clearly hadn't done much reading-up on the Scandinavian pop group,

RIGHT Björn and Agnetha with daughter Linda. Björn's lyrics for "Slipping through My Fingers" come from his sense of having missed parts of Linda's childhood.

ABOVE Agnetha fixes the tie of American talk show host Dick Cavett who was flown over to Sweden to interview the group for a TV special, *Dick Cavett Meets ABBA*, in April 1981

and seemed quite bemused as to why he'd ended up in a Swedish television studio. Also, the bantering and casual conversation that marked his talk shows in New York City were simply not the right framework for an ABBA interview. "As a group, our command of the English language wasn't such that we could have had an interesting and easy-going conversation," admitted Björn many years later. "It became a bit formal."

The nine-song concert was also a bit drab. Professional and well performed, certainly, but somehow lacking in energy and enthusiasm. The weird and wonderful stage costumes were long gone and the group now appeared in more sensible clothes, Björn looking like he'd simply picked something casual out of his wardrobe that morning; one reporter quipped

that with his green sleeveless jacket, he looked like a traveling salesman for fishing equipment. It was ABBA, but it was no longer the fun, slightly zany ABBA.

The television special, a co-production by Sweden's SVT and ZDF in West Germany, was always meant to be exported all over the world, but it seems global enthusiasm was rather low. Part of the problem was the lackluster and not particularly revealing conversation with Cavett. His shows were regularly imported and shown on Swedish television for most of the 1970s, but his international fame was perhaps not on the level ABBA and SVT had anticipated. Recalled Benny, "I think most countries said, 'Well, that's a nice show, but who's that guy? Why is he in the programme?' So that was a miscalculation."

Back in the recording studio, work continued as usual, ABBA as a musical unit seemingly unaffected by the marital splits, at least initially. "When the fuss died down it was actually a relief that we no longer had to keep up any pretence," explained Frida. "Once you're not involved emotionally it is much easier to work together. It becomes easier to concentrate. Everything is more efficient, because there is none of the blah-blah-blah—you just do your job and then go home. You don't get on each other's nerves when you don't see each other all the time."

Things were looking up for the two female members of ABBA on the romantic front as well. Frida had found a new boyfriend in Bertil "Bobo" Hjert, the owner of the highly successful poster manufacturer Scandecor; Bobo had been in her circle of friends for several years. Agnetha also entered into a long-term relationship in 1981, with a police inspector named Torbjörn Brander. She met him at her local police station in Lidingö, where she had gone to seek protection from a crazed fan who had been banging on her door at 3:30 in the morning, and then appeared outside the Polar studio a few days later. Mr Brander was the inspector in charge of the case; Agnetha said it was love at first sight. Before long they were engaged and he moved into her house, the relationship being revealed in the media in September 1981.

By that time, ABBA were still working on their new album, entitled *The Visitors*, sessions for which didn't conclude until November 15, just a couple of weeks before it reached the shops, on November 30. The album was a largely bleak affair, with little in the way of the upbeat hits the world had once fallen in love with. Only five years had passed since they sang "Dum Dum Diddle," but one could almost be forgiven for thinking that this was another group entirely. The subject matter included the then-current Cold War, with the ominous-sounding "Soldiers" constituting a warning against war, and the synthesizer psychedelia of the title track depicting the dangerous situation for dissidents in what was then the Soviet Union. Relationships gone wrong were explored in "When All Is Said and Done" and the Agnetha-led "One of Us," the latter being the only major hit single from the album, while the final track on side two, "Like an Angel Passing through My Room," a starkly arranged Frida-led reflection on a moment of stillness, brought the album journey to a somber close. Light relief, such as it was, came in the shape of "Head over Heels" and "Two for the Price of One," but one couldn't help feeling that ABBA's hearts really weren't in that kind of material anymore.

Reflected Frida, a decade after the album's release, "When you've gone through a separation, like all of us had done at that time, it puts a certain mood on the work, because then something disappeared that was so fundamental for the joy in our songs, that had always been there before. Even if the song itself was

> **66 Perhaps there was a bit of sadness or bitterness that coloured the making of that album. 99**
>
> Frida

downbeat, there was always a joy somewhere. But on *The Visitors* I believe we were all a bit tired of each other. We had already gone through so much together that there was no joy left. The recording became more of a routine experience. We had grown apart and began developing in different directions and the unity that had always been a part of our recordings was gone. I don't know—perhaps there was a bit of sadness or bitterness that coloured the making of that album." Nevertheless, although at the time the general public may have felt that Agnetha, Björn, Benny, and Frida weren't quite as fun and energetic as they used to be, in recent decades *The Visitors* has emerged as the connoisseur's favorite ABBA album, precisely because of its overt maturity and the darkness in many of its tracks.

The sleeve—shot in the atmospheric studio of the painter Julius Kronberg (1850–1921)—was also rather dark and bleak. For the first time on an album sleeve, the four members were completely separate from each other, signaling that ABBA really had turned from being a proper, close-knit group into a collective of independent individuals coming together from time to time. Album designer Rune Söderqvist claimed that the staging of the sleeve photo wasn't deliberate, but, clearly, the situation between the four members being what it was, he instinctively presented them this way.

Nor, it seems, did ABBA have very much time for promotional efforts. For the first time since they became famous, there were zero trips abroad to do television. If anyone wanted them on their shows, they had to travel to Stockholm and film them there. There were no performances of songs—the Dick Cavett special was supposed to take care of that for them—only sit-down interviews, and merely a handful of those. Outside the recording studio, ABBA just didn't feel very much like being ABBA anymore.

THE VISITORS

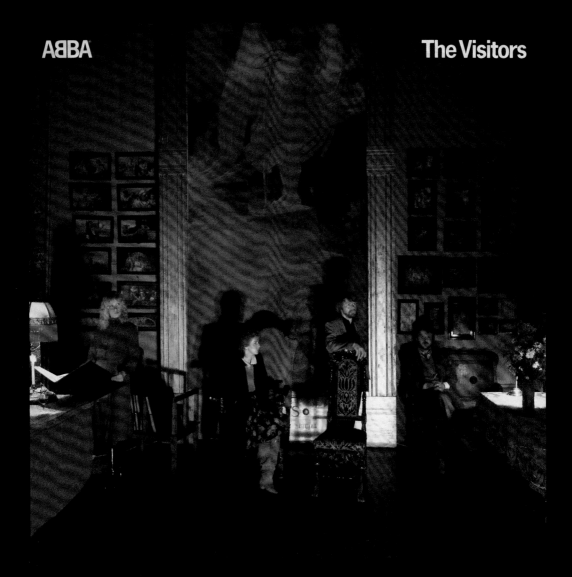

ABBA

The Visitors

SIDE ONE

The Visitors
Head over Heels
When All Is Said and Done
Soldiers

SIDE TWO

I Let the Music Speak
One of Us
Two for the Price of One
Slipping through My Fingers
Like an Angel Passing through
  My Room

Recorded: Polar Music Studio, Stockholm, Sweden

Produced and arranged by: Benny Andersson and Björn Ulvaeus

Engineered by: Michael B. Tretow

Personnel:
Agnetha Fältskog: vocals
Anni-Frid Lyngstad: vocals
Björn Ulvaeus: vocals, guitar, mandolin
Benny Andersson: vocals, keyboards
Lasse Wellander: guitar, mandolin
Rutger Gunnarsson: bass, mandolin
Ola Brunkert, Per Lindvall: drums
Åke Sundqvist: percussion
Janne Kling: flute, clarinet

Cover art:
Rune Söderqvist: layout
Lars Larsson: photography

Released: November 30, 1981 (UK release date: December 11, 1981; US release date: December 1981)

Label: Polar POLS 342

Notes
The Visitors is the only ABBA album where there are solo lead vocals in the verses of each and every song, in a marked contrast to songs such as "Mamma Mia" and "Dancing Queen," which Agnetha and Frida sang in unison. Björn later explained that this was because the lyrics had become more personal. "I felt that the lyrics had suddenly become more real to me. I could 'hear' what they were singing, whereas in the early days that hadn't mattered as much. To have two voices singing these kinds of lyrics was completely unnatural to me."

WE CAN'T GO
ON FOREVER

We Can't Go On Forever

As most of those within ABBA's inner circle knew, the dream of one day writing a musical had been on Björn and Benny's mind for a long time. Inspired by productions such as Andrew Lloyd Webber and Tim Rice's *Jesus Christ Superstar*, and perhaps also rock operas in the vein of The Who's *Tommy*, the thought of trying something similar had cropped up regularly over the years.

The Girl with the Golden Hair, the so-called mini-musical featured in ABBA's 1977 concert tour, was a first step. After that, there had been a few announcements that the two songwriters were going to set aside a year to write a larger, cohesive work, one example being the New Year's Eve musical they had tried to get John Cleese interested in. A year later, just before they began sessions for what was to become *The Visitors*, Benny hinted that the new album would probably be more conceptual. "That makes it a little different, because you can fit in things that normally wouldn't go with an album as separate tracks. If all the tracks are related to each other, it makes a whole of everything." As usual, those plans came to naught. Part of the problem was that although they had more than enough musical talent, they were well aware they needed to work with someone who had a better grasp of storytelling than they did.

Toward the end of 1981, there was a promising development on that end. Lyricist Tim Rice, no longer working with Andrew Lloyd Webber, was searching for new composers to collaborate with. Through mutual connections in the United States, Rice learned that the Andersson/Ulvaeus team was looking for someone to collaborate with. A meeting was set up in Stockholm in December 1981 and the three men found that they got

on like a house on fire. The message from Rice was that whenever they felt they had time to work with him, he would be ready and willing.

At the beginning of 1982, however, Björn and Benny had other things on their mind. In January, within a week of each other, they both became parents again; Björn and Lena had a daughter they named Emma, while Benny and Mona's son would be named Ludvig. Both songwriters had resolved to take a few months off once their children were born, and they were true to their promise. This left the female half of ABBA with nothing in particular to do, and while Agnetha spent time with her children, Frida took the opportunity to try something outside the group.

After her marital split in 1981, Frida's daughter, Lise-Lotte, had played Phil Collins's *Face Value* album to her. Largely the result of a divorce, Collins's album, which featured the big hit "In the Air Tonight," struck a chord with Frida and she played little else for several months afterwards. Now she was determined that Collins should produce her album. He agreed and sessions at Polar Music Studio were penciled in between mid-February and early April 1982. For Frida, stepping out of the security provided by ABBA in general and Benny in particular for the first time in a decade was an experience fraught with nerves and insecurity. Recalled Collins, "The first week she was, 'I don't know, what do *you* think?' but I said, 'Listen, it's your album, baby, it's not mine.' And after two or three weeks, she really started to come through."

Issued in September as *Something's Going On*, the album spawned one proper hit single, the Russ Ballard-penned "I Know There's Something Going On"—produced and arranged in much the same way as "In the Air Tonight"—which went Top Twenty in the United States and Top Five in Australia. Frida would look back on this result with unabashed pride

PAGE 160 ABBA, 1982

OPPOSITE ABBA meet Tim Rice and his wife Jane Artereta London, UK, 1982

as she herself had chosen this particular song from the hundreds of selections submitted to her when the album was put together. Toward the end of the sessions Björn and Benny were trying to come up with something—it was Stig Anderson, trusting few others to come up with hit material, who insisted that they contribute to the album—but, ultimately, no song of theirs appeared on it. Frida was secretly relieved. "They didn't get anything out until the album was almost completed," she explained later that year. "I decided not to use anything from them. Now I think it was a wise decision. It is good not to have the members of the group involved in this project." As she was trying to establish a new identity for herself it was important for

BELOW Frida with Phil Collins (L) who produced her solo album *Something's Going On*, 1982

RIGHT Frida's first solo single post-ABBA, "I Know There's Something Going On"

OPPOSITE Frida, 1982

Frida that *Something's Going On* was about her and her alone.

Agnetha was also starting to consider projects outside the group. The previous year, she had released a Swedish-language Christmas album with her daughter, Linda, and in August 1982 she devoted a few weeks to her first dramatic film role. *Raskenstam* was a movie about a real-life lonely-hearts racketeer in 1930s Sweden, helmed by Swedish actor and director Gunnar Hellström, who also played the titular lead role. Agnetha appeared as Lisa Mattsson, one of the many women the title character swindles. She certainly didn't have to be ashamed of her contribution, which added up to a convincingly human characterization. "In everything else I've done I've been Agnetha of ABBA," she said, "but when I watched the movie I saw another person: I saw Lisa." Opening in Sweden in August 1983, *Raskenstam* was quite successful, but although Agnetha would receive further offers she never again did any screen acting.

And now that all four members were starting to engage in outside activities, or at least ponder the possibilities, what about ABBA? The year had started with a major question mark, when they issued the second single from *The Visitors*. "Head over Heels" wanted to be one of those happy, energetic songs that had once brought the group global fame, but somehow missed the mark; as Björn would later admit, "It doesn't quite get there." ABBA regarded Britain as the barometer of what was hot and what was not in contemporary pop music, so their jaws must have dropped when "Head over Heels" climbed no higher than No. 25 in the UK, the first time a single of theirs had stalled outside the Top Ten since "I Do, I Do, I Do, I Do, I Do" in 1975. It did better in a handful of European countries, but somehow that success didn't carry quite the same weight as far as ABBA were concerned.

When Björn and Benny finally emerged from their paternity leave to start working on the next ABBA album, something seemed to be not quite right. Sessions kicked off on May 3, 1982, but about a month later everything ground to a halt. Three songs had been completed—"You Owe Me One," "Just Like That," and "I Am the City"—but although Agnetha was really fond of "Just Like That," Björn and Benny weren't particularly happy with any of the tracks in their present state. More worryingly, they didn't feel motivated to face the challenge head-on and soldier

OPPOSITE Agnetha makes her film debut with Gunnar Hellstrom in the romantic comedy *Raskenstam*

> **❝I don't think I've ever experienced such a bad atmosphere in a recording studio. It wasn't exactly cordial. ❞**
>
> Janne Schaffer

on with the album, like they would have just a year earlier. "Without actually putting it into words among ourselves, I guess we hadn't exactly run out of steam, but there was something that wasn't like it used to be," recalled Björn several decades later. "We didn't feel that same kind of strong spirit, and perhaps a feeling was starting to creep in that ABBA couldn't go on forever." So, instead of continuing work on the album, just a couple of weeks after this first batch of sessions concluded, there was an announcement that there would be no new studio LP in 1982. Instead, the group would take a summer break, then return to the studio to record a handful of new songs and issue a double album of their biggest hit singles in chronological order, with two of the new songs—also to be released as single A-sides—included on it.

On August 2, ABBA were back at Polar Music Studios, kicking off a month-long series of sessions for the songs they needed for the double album. Depending on who you ask, everything was working just as smoothly in the studio between the four members as it had always done, or something fundamental had changed. Janne Schaffer—a guitarist who had worked with ABBA throughout their career—had been absent from the group's recordings for a couple of years, but was present for the August 1982 sessions. He was astonished by the change of mood when Agnetha and Frida came to the studio to try out the keys. "I don't think I've ever experienced such a bad atmosphere in a recording studio. It wasn't exactly cordial. Everything was dealt with really quickly and tersely, it was all very correct: 'That sounds nice. Good luck, guys.' It wasn't, 'Wow, this is really cool!' You felt a lack of commitment from the ladies." Björn later admitted that although there had been a feeling of relief immediately after the divorces, the dynamics had changed in a way that sometimes made things more difficult. "I guess it could be frosty sometimes," he told interviewer Jim Irvin.

"It was harder to say, Please do that again. [Without someone saying] 'No, I don't want to!'"

Three songs were completed during the August 1982 sessions. First up were the Agnetha-led "Under Attack" and Frida's solo number "Cassandra," neither of which were terribly exciting tracks. The third and final song was decidedly more interesting. The tune for "The Day Before You Came" was written in the studio, something that Björn and Benny rarely indulged in. But they probably felt they were running out of time, yet needed to come up with something quickly, before Frida went abroad in September to promote her solo album.

Benny had an idea for a tune and played it, as he remembered, "out of the blue," on his Yamaha GX-1 synthesizer. A complete melody soon took shape, and since they had no musicians in the studio, they decided to make do with a drum machine and let Benny play everything else (they later brought in a real live drummer to beef up the sound a bit). Björn—by now an astute lyricist with a keen understanding of how to combine words and music so that they sounded like a natural fit—came up with lyrics wherein a woman chronicles all the dull, ordinary things she "guessed she must have done" the day before she had an emotionally charged encounter with a man. "I wrote down all the everyday incidents and things I could think of, that would happen to someone leading a routine kind of life. It was very difficult from a grammatical point of view to get it all to fit together, because it would all have to be logical, there was no room for hitches. The lyrics are not an actual story, but rather one big reflection on everything that 'must have' happened the day before this guy came. It must have been so incredibly boring, such a meagre existence, in the light of this amazing thing that happened then."

Agnetha was assigned the lead vocals on "The Day Before You Came" and was instructed to do a straightforward performance, truly inhabiting the character of the woman in the song. Her way into the song was through "imitation," something that had worked well for her before (for example, borrowing some inflections from late-1950s American singer Connie Francis to find the right sentimental tone in the Waterloo album's "Hasta Mañana"). "I had an idea that, 'I'm trying to sing this as [French balladeer] Charles Aznavour would have done.' So I said, 'Let me try that' and I did, and it came out very, very special." Frida pitched in with an "operatic" wordless obbligato line, as if sung by a spectral presence watching the sad events taking place.

There was even something melancholy in the air during the vocal session, at least according to engineer Michael Tretow. He recalled that Agnetha recorded her lead vocal with the lights down, creating a special mood in the studio. "That was a magical and rather sad experience, because it really felt like this is the last ABBA song we're ever going to make. [You could feel it] in the studio. And the lyrics are so touching, so everybody had a lump in their throat while we were doing that song."

Released as a single in October 1982, "The Day Before You Came" reached the Top Five in a number of European countries, but continued ABBA's downhill slide in the UK, getting no further than No. 32 on the singles chart. As brilliant as it was, "The Day Before You Came" didn't really sound like a hit single, and if ABBA had had more tracks to choose from—as they would have if they'd been recording a studio album—maybe they would have selected something with more immediate catchiness. This slightly middle-aged, low-key piece of art perhaps wasn't what UK singles buyers wanted when they were in the process of falling in love with colorful "new pop" phenomena such as Boy George, whose group Culture Club achieved its breakthrough with "Do You Really Want to Hurt Me" around this time.

The double album compilation, The Singles—The First Ten Years, issued on November 8, fared better in the UK, going all the way to No. 1, giving the group their eighth consecutive album chart-topper; it did reasonably well in other markets as well. ABBA promoted the album and its attendant singles with visits to the UK and West Germany, also being interviewed on Swedish TV. The UK TV appearance, on BBC TV's The Late Late Breakfast show, where they were interviewed by Noel Edmonds, came off as pretty awkward, as if the four members no longer quite knew how to interact with each other in a context which was based on tongue-in-cheek quips and cheery banter. A joke Benny cracked at Frida's expense, that was meant to be light-hearted—the subtext being, "see, everything is still fine between us!"—came off as him being rude to her. The Swedish interview was much better: No probing questions, perhaps, but all four appeared more relaxed, and somehow relieved not to have to live up to any other expectations than being four individuals.

The second single from the compilation album, "Under Attack," fared just slightly better in the UK than "The Day Before You Came," reaching No. 26, but performed rather dismally in most other places. In

Australia, it "peaked" at No. 96, which was as good an illustration as any that the days of intense, all-consuming Abbamania down under were long gone.

During their London visit something happened that was more important for ABBA's future than their uncomfortable Noel Edmonds interview. After Björn and Benny had discussed their plans for a musical on and off during the year, they met up with Tim Rice again and agreed that the three of them really were going to do something together. The decision was toasted with champagne. At first, there were plans to write the musical parallel with work on a new ABBA album, but before long those highly impractical plans

ABOVE An awkward interview on *The Late Late Breakfast Show*

were shelved. Instead, ABBA would take a break and, when Björn and Benny had completed their musical, they could get back together—if they felt like it.

On December 11, 1982, ABBA made a second appearance on *The Late Late Breakfast Show*, this time via satellite from a Stockholm television studio, being interviewed by Noel Edmonds and performing "Under Attack" and "I Have a Dream."' This not very monumental television appearance turned out to be the last thing they did together in public. Just like Michael Tretow had suspected, "The Day Before You Came" really was ABBA's last recording. No one knew it for certain at the time, but when the cameras were switched off and Agnetha, Björn, Benny, and Frida left the television studio on that December night, the ABBA story was over.

ABBA, 1982. The last studio session

THE FIRST
TEN YEARS

SIDE ONE

Ring Ring
Waterloo
So Long
I Do, I Do, I Do, I Do, I Do
SOS
Mamma Mia
Fernando

SIDE TWO

Dancing Queen
Money, Money, Money
Knowing Me, Knowing You
The Name of the Game
Take a Chance on Me
Summer Night City

SIDE THREE

Chiquitita
Does Your Mother Know
Voulez-Vous
Gimme! Gimme! Gimme!
   (A Man after Midnight)
I Have a Dream

SIDE FOUR

The Winner Takes It All
Super Trouper
One of Us
The Day Before You Came
Under Attack

Cover art:
Rune Söderqvist: layout
Lars Larsson: photography

Released: November 8, 1982 (UK release date:
November 5, 1982; US release date: December 1982)

Label: Polar POLMD 400/401

Notes
The number of tracks on the album was originally going
to be twenty-six, but because of the limited space
available in the vinyl days there were only twenty-three
tracks on the released version. It's not known exactly
which three tracks were left off, but they may have been
"People Need Love," "Honey, Honey," and "Eagle.'"
Even twenty-three tracks was a bit of a stretch, and so,
to cut the running time, a shorter promotional edit of
"The Name of the Game" was included instead of the
original hit single version.

FANTASY AND FREEDOM

Fantasy And Freedom

With ABBA going on hiatus, the members had to consider what else they could do with their lives. Björn and Benny had their time pretty much sewn up with their musical, while Frida was still promoting her *Something's Going On* album and also adjusting to her new life as a resident of London, where she had moved at the end of 1982. Her relocation was a part of the continued reinvention of herself after the split from Benny, but also a consequence of no longer feeling comfortable in Sweden because of the constant speculation on her love life in the press. "When Benny and I divorced it was really hard for me," she remembered, "because if I appeared in public, as a private person at a party, for instance, and a man happened to stand beside me or behind me, he was immediately labelled as 'Frida's new man.' With my strong sense of integrity . . . I thought this was dreadful. I found it hard to accept that I would be described as a kind of person I didn't recognise." Creating a new base for herself, she also began planning for her next solo album; she hoped Phil Collins would return as producer.

Agnetha, meanwhile, began sessions for her first English-language solo album at Polar Music Studios in January 1983. Her chosen producer was Mike Chapman, who rose to fame in the 1970s in his partnership with Nicky Chinn as songwriters behind hits for The Sweet, Mud, Suzi Quatro, and Smokie, and latterly making a name for himself as a US-based producer, achieving major success with acts such as The Knack and Blondie. The album, released as *Wrap Your Arms around Me* in May 1983, was conceived in much the same way as Frida's album: Songwriters were invited to contribute material, while other selections were found in music publishers' drawers. It all added up to a well-produced if slightly anonymous album, which nevertheless was a huge hit in Sweden and performed reasonably well in most other countries, selling around 1.2 million copies. Its success was helped along by the buoyant, calypso-flavored lead-off single, "The Heat Is On," a marked contrast to the sad songs that had come to constitute Agnetha's main repertoire in ABBA. Agnetha also scored a Top Thirty hit in the United States with the rocky "Can't Shake Loose," written by Russ Ballard, who'd also penned Frida's "I Know There's Something Going On."

Ever fearful of flying, Agnetha preferred traveling by bus on her promotional trips. On one such journey from London, late one night in October 1983, she was involved in a serious accident as the bus arrived in Sweden. "The bus began to sway violently from side to side," she recalled. "There were screeching brakes and upset voices. I was thrown around and hit myself hard on the head and legs. The moments when I first realised we were having an accident were frightening. I couldn't see anything because I was back in the sleeping compartment. But I do remember the last awful thump when we overturned and spun around, and the crashing of glass." Holding on to her mattress, Agnetha flew through a broken window, ending up in a ditch. Everyone on the bus survived, with only minor injuries, which must count as something of a miracle given the seriousness of the crash. But the gossip press speculation that Agnetha had been pregnant as the crash happened—she wasn't—did nothing to strengthen her resolve to remain in the public spotlight.

Björn and Benny had their hands full with *Chess*, their musical collaboration with Tim Rice. Spending most of 1983 recording demos, the following year was mainly devoted to recording the concept album that would be the first manifestation of the work. The premise of the musical was the game of chess used as a metaphor

PAGE 174 ABBA, France, 1980
OPPOSITE Agnetha, 1983

> ## " I don't want to be a part of this anymore. I want to devote myself to music, not to business. "
>
> Benny

for a love story, as well as the East–West relationship during the Cold War years. Rice, who'd been kicking the idea around since the mid-1970s, had found much of his inspiration for the concept in the 1972 World Chess Championship match between Bobby Fischer and Boris Spassky in Reykjavik, Iceland. In *Chess*, the male lead of The Russian was played by Swedish singer Tommy Körberg, while Murray Head took on the role of The American. British musical star Elaine Paige was Florence, the American player's second who falls in love with the Russian, and singer Barbara Dickson was the Russian's wife, Svetlana.

For Björn and Benny, the latter part of the ABBA years had sometimes been marked by a desire to break free from the constraints of what a "pop" album should be about. One of the *Chess* musical's showstoppers, the Tommy Körberg-sung "Anthem," was a case in point: It had cropped up in songwriting sessions since the mid-1970s, but was always felt to be not pop enough. On the other hand, there were tracks such as "I Let the Music Speak" on *The Visitors*, structured like a musical number and encompassing different "movements," that they somehow couldn't help themselves from recording with ABBA. With *Chess*, they were completely free to include whatever piece of music they wanted, just as long as it was appropriate for the story they were trying to tell.

Such was the close collaboration between Björn, Benny, and Tim Rice that they credited the musical to all three, without the usual "music by"/"lyrics by" division, although Andersson/Ulvaeus were mainly responsible for the music, while Rice was in charge of the words. Nevertheless, it wasn't as if an accomplished lyricist like Björn wouldn't have anything of value to contribute. "[Björn] used to give me lyrics which were meant to be nonsense lyrics, but they always had wonderful lines in them, which I was able to nick and save myself many hours of pain," said Tim Rice, pointing in particular to the line "One night in Bangkok makes a hard man

humble" from "One Night in Bangkok." "I have been told by so many people that this was a complete summary of my brilliance—but Björn wrote it!"

Issued in October 1984, ahead of the stage premiere in May 1986, and promoted by a brief European tour, the *Chess* double album was a virtual smorgasbord of different musical styles, from pop/rock to pieces heavily influenced by operetta and classical music. Working within such a lofty and overtly aspirational area had been Björn and Benny's ultimate goal for several years, and once they got there it sometimes added up to—dare one say it—a somewhat pretentious experience. The reviews were generally positive, though, in some respects more so than for any of the ABBA albums. It went on to sell two million copies, which must count as successful for such a release, the reviews and the commercial success strengthening Björn and Benny's feeling that they had been right to attempt a musical. *Chess* also yielded two major hit singles in the Elaine Paige and Barbara Dickson duet "I Know Him So Well," which spent four weeks at No. 1 in the UK, and Murray Head's rap number "One Night in Bangkok," a No. 3 hit in the US, a better chart position than any of ABBA's singles except "Dancing Queen" and "Take a Chance on Me." Incidentally, the chorus of "I Know Him So Well" was lifted from a song entitled "I Am an A," which ABBA had performed during their 1977 tour as a way of introducing the four members to the audience. There were other examples of tunes or melody fragments in *Chess* that had been around since the ABBA days.

With the success of *Chess*, 1984 ended on a high note for Björn and Benny. There were also other changes afoot for the pair. In November, long-time Anglophile Björn followed in Frida's footsteps and moved to the UK with his wife and youngest daughter, settling in Henley-on-Thames, Oxfordshire, famously also the home of ex-Beatle George Harrison. In conjunction with the move he sold all his interests in Polar Music International, as did Benny at the same time.

The past couple of years had seen a gulf growing between the Andersson/Ulvaeus team and Stig Anderson. Where once the trio had worked closely in their quest of bringing Swedish pop music to the world, Stig had become much more involved in the business side of things while Björn and Benny had felt increasingly annoyed at the way Polar's investment ventures obscured the company's core business of making credible pop music. One example was the 1982 purchase of a Swedish investment company: After fluctuating wildly on the stock market, it was ultimately sold in October 1983 at a considerable monetary loss

ABOVE Benny (L) and Bjorn (R) with Stig Anderson in 1984

to Stig, Björn, Benny, and Agnetha; Frida had sold her shares in the investment company when she moved to London at the end of 1982, and was fortunate enough that their value was very high at that point. At the same time, she also rid herself of all shares in Polar Music International, with Agnetha following suit a year later. And now Björn and Benny also sold out.

The first outward signs that things weren't like they used to be came when Björn and Benny ensured that Stig and Polar were not formally involved in the *Chess* project, instead forming a separate company with Tim Rice and then licensing the double album to Polar. Although the *Chess* agreement included the rights to negotiate a worldwide deal with RCA, the exclusion must have been hurtful to Stig, who, during the ABBA years, had mentioned several times in the press the plans of the musical that "we" were going to write.

Even before ABBA came into being, their manager was a well-known and outspoken personality in

Sweden. In the politicized 1970s, Stig was constantly at loggerheads with those who criticized ABBA for being so overtly commercial. He also had a knack for telling the press exactly what Polar and ABBA were going to do with their money, and as he tended to use the word "we" in interviews—meaning him and ABBA—an impression was created that Agnetha, Björn, Benny, and Frida were behind everything Stig said and did. Coupled with his sudden outbursts of anger, which employees at Polar and Sweden Music had come to take as par for the course, it added up to a person that, for all his achievements and positive character traits, could be difficult to handle.

Now that Björn and Benny finally severed all ties to Polar, Stig tried to be diplomatic in his comments, but his former protégés were more forthright. "We are on separate paths professionally," said Björn. "We were different even when we first got together, and it's not like we've grown closer over the years." Explained Benny, "I don't want to be a part of this anymore. I want to devote myself to music, not to business."

In early October 1984, virtually the moment Björn and Benny vacated Polar Music Studios after completing *Chess*, Agnetha entered the main studio for a month of sessions for her second English-language album, *Eyes of a Woman*. This time the producer was Eric Stewart, formerly of 1970s hit band 10cc. Released in the spring of 1985, the album virtually screamed mid-1980s in terms of production aesthetics. Agnetha herself contributed the most hit-like song on the album, the super-catchy "I Won't Let You Go," featuring lyrics by Stewart; it was the lead-off single from the album, hitting the Top Ten in Sweden. But as she admitted around this time, songwriting had become something of a chore for her, a marked contrast to the early part of her career when the tunes were flowing out of her. "Do you realise how hard it is to compose? It's so boring!" she told a reporter. "It might be easier for those who work in pairs, but I was struggling alone with 'I Won't Let

You Go' for the whole of last summer. It's only a matter of hard work, no glamour at all." The album otherwise largely consisted of songs submitted by publishers and Eric Stewart's friends, adding up to yet another professional-sounding but slightly impersonal release. Agnetha didn't do very much promotion for it, annoying Stewart by saying no to high-profile talk shows in the UK, and the album didn't do much business except in Sweden and one or two European countries.

Career-wise, Frida was doing even worse. Her second post-ABBA solo album, *Shine*, was ultimately not produced by Phil Collins, but by producer-du-jour Steve Lillywhite, who'd risen to fame after collaborations with acts such as Peter Gabriel, U2, and Simple Minds. Recorded in Paris in the spring of 1984, *Shine* was issued in September of that year. For the first time ever, Frida had attempted songwriting, and her tender ballad "Don't Do It" was included on

the album. But *Shine* only went Top Ten in Sweden, where an album by a former ABBA member was expected to automatically peak nearer the top. None of its singles were hits of note anywhere, and the album died a dismal death. Frida, who was really proud of what she and Lillywhite had achieved, feeling that she had been successful in her attempt at placing herself smack in the middle of contemporary pop-rock, was taken aback. Perhaps the main problem was the gulf between what the public expected from a former ABBA member and Frida's attempt at reinvention, ultimately pleasing no one except her most ardent fans.

OPPOSITE Agnetha pictured with producer Eric Stewart (L) and sound engineer Paris Edvinsson (R), 1984

ABOVE Frida in the studio with producer Steve Lillywhite (L), Paris, 1984

At the time of *Shine*'s release, she said she was already writing songs for her next album. But following the flop, Frida re-evaluated her life completely, realizing that what she really needed was to establish an existence that had nothing to do with show business. Her romance with Bobo Hjert had ended in 1984, but soon afterwards she met and fell in love with Ruzzo Reuss von Plauen, a real-life prince, setting up home with him in Switzerland. Frida withdrew from the music business—many years later, she would mention the need to "heal" after all she had been through during the ABBA years—and for the remainder of the 1980s would only make sporadic ventures to the recording studio, guesting on other people's records.

In May 1986, after a number of setbacks, *Chess* finally received its stage opening in London's West End. Reviews were mixed, but the show did well, running for almost three years at the Prince Edward Theatre.

A Broadway opening in 1988 was less successful: The plot had been identified as the main weakness of *Chess*, and so a new manuscript was written for it. It didn't help the production, which received devastatingly bad reviews and closed after only two months. On the night of the opening, after the reviews came in, Björn, ABBA's dedicated full-time worrier, suffered chest pains and was rushed to hospital with a suspected heart attack. The *Chess* flop in New York was the first major setback Björn and Benny had

experienced in their careers. Outside the unforgiving world of Broadway, however, the show would live on, being performed in concert innumerable times, and also being staged regularly in many different countries over the decades.

And what about ABBA? After all, when they took their break so that Björn and Benny could concentrate on their musical, the agreement was that they would get back together again if they felt like it. For the first couple of years, comments from some of the members

past when the future looked as if it would offer more interesting challenges?

In January 1986, Stig Anderson was the subject of a *This Is Your Life* program on Swedish television, with the ABBA members recording a light-hearted video where they did a slightly shambolic performance of Stig's first hit, "Tivedshambo." This would mark the last time for several decades that Agnetha, Björn, Benny, and Frida would be seen together in public. Notably, the members had not planned on appearing on the live broadcast of *This Is Your Life*, indicating that none of them felt especially close to Stig any longer. Björn and Benny were ultimately persuaded to show up, making for a somewhat awkward segment where the less than cordial relationship between the songwriters and their former manager and business partner was evident.

Later that year, in August, after many years of requests from fans, Polar Music released an album entitled *ABBA Live*. The group itself didn't quite see the point of live albums, arguing that it's "boring to hear 'reproductions' of songs that sound much better in the studio," as Björn phrased it. Eventually, they relented, but kept the project at arm's length: Michael B. Tretow mixed the album, and Rune Söderqvist designed it, but the ABBA members were not involved. As if to underline that ABBA's time had been and gone, the album performed badly upon release. In Sweden, it spent two weeks at No. 49 before dropping out of the album chart. Most elsewhere, *ABBA Live* didn't chart at all, and in ABBA-crazy UK, they didn't even release it. The 1980s-flavored mix and the fact that ABBA themselves didn't really care about it seemed to conspire to put people off the album.

ABBA may have been a thing of the past, but Björn and Benny still wanted to go on making pop records. Forming a partnership with brother-and-sister duo Anders and Karin Glenmark (both had been heavily involved in the *Chess* concept album and subsequent tour), in 1985 they issued an album entitled *Gemini*, which also became the name of the duo. The album did reasonably well in Sweden, but didn't make much noise elsewhere. A second album, issued in 1987, *Geminism*, was met with equal indifference. The songs were as tuneful as you'd expect from Björn and Benny, but the public didn't respond to the singers, and that second album proved to be the last.

were rather optimistic, indicating that there was no reason they couldn't continue as ABBA. But *Chess*—double album and London stage production—took much longer to see through than anticipated, and by the time Björn and Benny were free again, none of the members was interested anymore. Frida had left the music business; Agnetha was feeling less and less motivated to go on making records; and Björn and Benny had been encouraged by the success of *Chess*—what was the point of going back to the

Instead, later in 1987, Benny issued his first solo album, *Klinga mina klockor* ("Ring, My Bells"), mainly consisting of tunes in the Swedish folk tradition. He had not expected any great sales for the album, and was surprised to see it climb to No. 6 and spend twenty weeks on the chart. Benny had underestimated the Swedish public's love for his music and the fact that, as a composer, he was turning into something of a national treasure, many of his melodies capturing something essentially Swedish. A second album, *November 1989*, also did well.

OPPOSITE Benny with son Ludvig in 1985
BELOW Agnetha, 1988

Agnetha, meanwhile, issued no less than two albums in 1987. The first was a children's album with her son, Christian, but later in the year came the Peter Cetera-produced *I Stand Alone*. As with her previous albums, it was hugely successful in Sweden, spending eight weeks at No. 1, but barely registered elsewhere. A minimum of promotion was conducted, but after Agnetha had appeared on BBC TV's *Wogan* in February 1988, it would take more than fifteen years before she appeared on live TV again. There was talk of a follow-up album, but instead Agnetha quietly disappeared from view and was rarely heard or seen over the following decade. Life as a public figure, whether promoting new music or being the subject of endless gossip-rag stories, had lost all its attraction. Like Frida, Agnetha needed to find a new identity for herself.

ABBA LIVE

SIDE ONE

Dancing Queen
Take a Chance on Me
I Have a Dream
Does Your Mother Know
Chiquitita

SIDE TWO

Thank You for the Music
Two for the Price of One
Fernando
Gimme! Gimme! Gimme!
  (A Man after Midnight)
Super Trouper
Waterloo

EXTRA TRACKS ON CD

Money, Money, Money
The Name of the Game/Eagle
On and On and On

Cover art:
Rune Söderqvist: layout
J. Geary: drawing
Anders Hanser: photography

Released: August 18, 1986 (UK release date: April 9, 1992; US release date: September 1986)

Label: Polar POLS 412/POLCD 412.

Notes

Most of the tracks on *ABBA Live* were taken from the group's concerts at Wembley Arena in November 1979, the exceptions being "Fernando" and "Money, Money, Money," recorded in Australia in March 1977, and the April 1981 *Dick Cavett Meets ABBA* selections "Two for the Price of One," "Gimme! Gimme! Gimme! (A Man after Midnight)," "Super Trouper," and "On and On and On."

AN EXTRAORDINARY
COMEBACK

An Extraordinary Comeback

"They received every single penny they should have," said Stig Anderson in a 1997 interview, adding, with a sting of bitterness, "There is no gratitude in this world." Was he talking about some disgruntled business partners involved in one of Polar Music International's many investment schemes? No, Stig was directing his ire and disappointment at the four individuals in the group with which he had once worked closely to achieve global fame: ABBA.

The conflict between the group and their former manager had its roots in protracted contract negotiations between 1982 and 1984. The ABBA members were all part-owners of Polar Music International, but they also had a separate agreement as recording artists. This agreement, stipulating ABBA's royalty rates for record sales, needed to be adjusted, not least because there might come a time when none of the members were owners of Polar. In April 1984, after much haggling back and forth, there was finally an agreement that ABBA's royalty rate for sales outside Sweden would be adjusted from 3 to 9 percent. No contract was signed at the time, but there was a protocol from a meeting stating that ABBA should henceforth receive the higher royalty rate.

Five years later, in 1989, Stig Anderson—fifty-eight years old and no longer the energetic dynamo who'd journeyed from poverty to considerable wealth—decided to sell all his music business companies. None of his children were interested in taking over the business, so he had no choice but to find an outside buyer. Ultimately, an agreement was struck with the multinational music business giant Polygram.

PAGE 188 ABBA tribute group, Björn Again, featuring stage characters (L-R) Benny Anderwear, Frida Longstokin, Agnetha Falstart, and Björn Volvo-us, May 1991
OPPOSITE Björn (L) and Benny (R), c.1998

"The vibes haven't been the best between us . . . We don't have much contact."

Stig

As paperwork was gone through in preparation for Polygram's takeover, one of the ABBA members' business representatives discovered that the group's royalty rate had in fact not been adjusted to the terms of the April 1984 agreement: They were still on the same 3 percent deal. When confronted about this, Stig argued that the higher royalty had been dependent on the ABBA members getting back together and recording a new album. When that didn't happen, the royalty remained unchanged. ABBA's representatives maintained that there had been no such conditions in the agreement. When the parties failed to resolve the conflict, ABBA saw no other alternative than to file a lawsuit against Polar Music International.

The news about the conflict broke in July 1990, providing a sad coda to the glorious story of Stig and ABBA's remarkable achievement in making a Swedish pop group one of the world's biggest music business phenomena. Stig was convinced that he was in the right and was eager to have the case tried in court. However, Polygram, the new Polar owners, were more concerned that they should have good relations with the ABBA members, and wanted to avoid a public fight, so an out-of-court settlement was agreed upon. But the conflict killed any chances of Stig and ABBA ever becoming friends again: As Stig said in 1997, "the vibes haven't been the best between us since then. We don't have much contact." He would eventually patch things up with Frida, but relationships with the other group members remained frosty.

In the ABBA annals, it was certainly a depressing start to the new decade, but within a couple of years things would change for the better—to an extent that no one could have foreseen. While ABBA had been ignored for much of the 1980s, there was still a strong fan base out there. The music had been licensed out to labels specializing in budget releases, which said a lot about ABBA's perceived status at the time, but, on the quiet, the many shoddily packaged CDs that seemed to flood the market had been selling very well indeed. The cognoscenti may have regarded ABBA as an uncool 1970s joke dressed up in horrible costumes, but there were many, not very much bothered about what was cool or not, who still enjoyed their music.

As the most ardent fans—children and teenagers during ABBA's heyday—became adults, it also transpired that a high proportion of them were gay men. In the gay community, the ABBA revival started in the late 1980s as many of their fans were now in their twenties, and when they went out clubbing they wanted to hear the music they grew up with. ABBA ticked many of the boxes usually associated with gay male tastes—female lead singers with a touch of the regal diva (Frida) and the devastated woman facing all kinds of adversity (Agnetha); heartbreak ballads;

hedonistic disco in the vein of "Voulez-Vous" or "Gimme! Gimme! Gimme! (A Man after Midnight)"—so this development was not so surprising, although Björn and Benny would be forever puzzled as to why a group consisting of two heterosexual couples would be gay icons.

In the summer of 1992, synth duo Erasure—featuring gay lead singer Andy Bell—released their *Abba-esque* EP of ABBA covers. The EP gave them their only No. 1 on the UK singles chart, and it was also a major hit in many other countries. Videos for all four songs were made and in the one for "Take a Chance on Me," the duo camped it up, dressing up as Agnetha and Frida, underlining the gay culture angle. More pertinently, the success of *Abba-esque* also pointed up that the time may be right for an ABBA revival, already underlined by the many successful tribute bands that were popping up, the most successful at the time being Australia's Björn Again.

This was confirmed in September 1992, when Polygram released the compilation album *ABBA Gold*. The record company had waited for all of Polar's licensing deals across the world to run out before they started doing something with the catalog, and that time had finally come. In an effort to remove ABBA

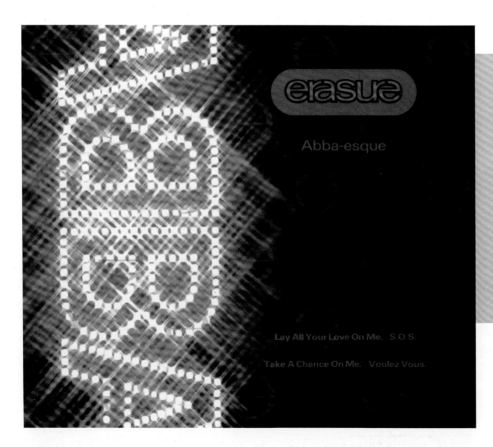

Abba-esque

Lay All Your Love On Me. S.O.S.

Take A Chance On Me. Voulez Vous.

66 **It's rather fantastic that the music is still around and that they didn't kill us for being so corny at the time.** 99

Benny

LEFT *Abba-esque* by Erasure, 1992

OPPOSITE Andy Bell, lead singer of Erasure, pays tribute to ABBA, Edinburgh Playhouse, Scotland, UK, 1992

from 1970s nostalgia and instead let the music be the star, the album was packaged simply, featuring just the title, prominently exposing the ABBA logo, against a black background, with no photo of the group. The results couldn't have been better. *ABBA Gold* hit No. 1 in several countries, and over the three decades since its release has kept on selling, its total sales figures now being well over thirty million. In the UK it is, at the time of writing, the only album to have spent more than a thousand weeks in the Top 100 albums chart.

Two Australian comedy films, both released in 1994, underlined ABBA's place in modern popular culture. *The Adventures of Priscilla, Queen of the Desert* explored the gay angle, following three drag queens on a journey across the desert, with plenty of ABBA

references in it. *Muriel's Wedding*, meanwhile, dealing with a girl who uses ABBA's music as an escape from life's hardships, opened the eyes of the world to the fact that ABBA had a strong emotional impact on people, going beyond the disposable pop tag that had been attached to them.

The extraordinary success of *ABBA Gold* meant that there had to be a follow-up, and in 1993 Polygram issued *More ABBA Gold*, a collection of hits that had to be left off *ABBA Gold* for space reasons, plus a few single B-sides and a slew of album tracks. The

ABOVE *The Adventures of Priscilla, Queen of the Desert*, 1994
OPPOSITE *Muriel's Wedding*, 1994

collection also featured a previously unreleased song, "I Am the City," from ABBA's aborted 1982 album sessions. It says something about the group's extraordinary comeback that this "part two" compilation album eventually notched up sales of more than two million copies, a lot more than most acts sell of their main compilations. In 1994, the obligatory 4-CD box set followed, again offering an overview of their hits and album tracks, and also a selection of previously unreleased recordings and session outtakes.

The former ABBA members watched their return to the public arena with some consternation, none of them truly expecting that their music would live on beyond being heard on oldies radio stations every now and then. For Björn and Benny, who were on a journey of development, writing dead-serious musicals and existing in a more high-brow environment, it was puzzling that so many people wanted to go back to that which they themselves felt they had outgrown. "We were extremely corny, I think," said Benny in 1992. "It's rather fantastic that the music is still around and that they didn't kill us for being so corny at the time."

Parallel with the ABBA revival, Björn and Benny were working on a new stage musical. By 1990, Björn and Lena had decided to move back to Sweden— in 1986, during their UK tenure, a second daughter, Anna, had been born—perhaps so that it would be easier for Björn and Benny to work together on such a large undertaking as a musical.

Based on a famous series of novels by Swedish

author Vilhelm Moberg, the work dealt with the hardships of Swedish immigrants to the United States in the late nineteenth century. Entitled *Kristina från Duvemåla* ("Kristina from Duvemåla") and opening in Malmö in the autumn of 1995, the musical was a major critical and commercial success. With its music largely based on Swedish folk music traditions, it also cemented Benny Andersson's status as a "national composer." *Kristina* was the first Andersson/Ulvaeus work credited as music: Andersson, lyrics: Ulvaeus, unlike the ABBA years when they always sat together writing the music. Benny had always been the main musical motor in the partnership, and the music/lyrics division had really begun back in the *Chess* days.

The musical moved on to Gothenburg and Stockholm, and when *Kristina från Duvemåla* finally closed in June 1999, more than one million people had seen it, in a country of less than nine million

people. Attempts to have it staged outside the Nordic countries were less successful, however. Workshops in New York City were followed by a couple of concert performances at Carnegie Hall in 2009, and then similar shows at London's Royal Albert Hall in 2010, but interest in staging such a bleak and "folky" story was minimal. The show, as appealing as it was to a large slice of the Swedish population, ran for more than three hours, and would be hard work for those who found it difficult to engage with the travails of the main characters.

The female half of ABBA kept a pretty low profile for the first half of the 1990s, although Frida emerged as an environmental campaigner of sorts. It all began when she read an article about acidification of forest soils, which made her feel like she had to do something about it. She started by founding an environmental organization called Artister för miljö ("Artists for the

Environment"). In the summer of 1992, Artister för miljö released a single in Sweden, featuring Frida singing Julian Lennon's "Saltwater," also organizing a concert in the courtyard of the Royal Palace of Stockholm. The King himself had given permission for a public event to be held in the courtyard, which was unique. Frida performed "Saltwater" and duetted with Marie Fredriksson of Roxette on the old Louis Armstrong hit "What a Wonderful World."

It wasn't entirely surprising that the King had given his permission. Through her relationship with Ruzzo Reuss, Frida had become friendly with the King and Queen of Sweden: Ruzzo's mother was Swedish, and as a teenager he had gone to the exclusive Lundsberg boarding school in Sweden, becoming friends with Sweden's future King Carl XVI Gustaf.

In August 1992, Frida and Ruzzo were finally married in a low-key ceremony at the church of Hørsholm in Denmark. As a result of the marriage, Frida formally acquired the title of Princess, though she claimed she never used it in everyday life. Her journey through life was nonetheless nothing less than remarkable, almost like a fairy tale, starting out as an outcast orphan child, then becoming a pop star, and finally ending up a bona fide Princess.

But what about her singing career? In 1996, she surprised the public by releasing her first album in twelve years. Notably, *Djupa andetag* ("Deep Breaths") was Swedish-language, as she didn't feel up to issuing an international album with all this would

OPPOSITE Björn (L) and Benny (R) work together on musical *Kristina från Duvemåla* ("Kristina from Duvemåla"), 1995

BELOW Benny plays accordion onstage with Swedish folkmusic group Orsa Spelmän, 1996

entail in terms of publicity and the need for promotional trips. The album was meant to reflect the fifty-year-old woman she was, with producer Anders Glenmark—emerging as a successful recording artist after his time in Gemini—providing most of the music and lyrics, channeling her thoughts and emotions. *Djupa andetag* was a big hit in Sweden, reaching No. 1 and selling more than 100,000 copies.

Around the same time, Agnetha had a re-emergence of sorts, after hardly being seen or heard from in more than eight years. Despite her low-key existence, though, those years had been dramatic enough. Agnetha's engagement to police inspector Torbjörn Brander had

been broken off in 1984, after which she had been linked with one or two other men. In December 1990, there was suddenly an announcement that she had married surgeon Tomas Sonnenfeld, but less than two years later, in November 1992, the couple filed for divorce. Then, in January 1994, her mother, Birgit, passed away, while her father died in December 1995, their final years having been marked by ill health. "I

ABOVE Frida, now Princess Reuss, with husband Prince Heinrich Ruzzo Reuss of Plauen, whom she married in August 1992

OPPOSITE Agnetha, 1998

think of the last few years and they haven't been kind to me," Agnetha said, reflecting on her turbulent first half of the decade. "The loneliness weighs heavy upon me."

That interview quote came from an official book written about her by friend and confidante, journalist Brita Åhman. The book had been long in the making: It was in the works back in 1983, but following Agnetha's bus crash and the speculation that followed in the press, she lost interest. However, with the ABBA revival came more writings that Agnetha felt were either gossipy or inaccurate or both, and so she said yes when Brita suggested that they should revive the project. Here was a chance to set the record straight. Published

❝ I think of the last few years and they haven't been kind to me. ❞

Agnetha

in Swedish in 1996, followed by an English edition in 1997, the book, entitled *As I Am*, was something of a disappointment. It wasn't without its nuggets of interesting information and reflections on Agnetha's life, but much of the slim volume consisted of Åhman's narration, and one couldn't help getting the impression that most of Agnetha's energy had gone into deciding what she didn't want to talk about, rather than sharing her memories and insights in any greater detail.

In conjunction with the book, a double CD covering her career as a recording artist was released in Sweden, titled *My Love, My Life* after the ABBA ballad first heard on the *Arrival* album. It was a nice enough chronicle of her career, but peaked outside the Top Twenty. Similarly, the book received bad reviews and achieved disappointing sales, no doubt partly because Agnetha did nothing to promote either the book or the double CD. After these releases, all went quiet again.

While the ABBA revival rolled on and his former protégés were back in the spotlight again, Stig Anderson had become increasingly withdrawn and was suffering deteriorating health. In the mid-1980s, he and Gudrun divorced after she discovered he was having an affair with another woman. They eventually patched things up, but they never remarried. Stig had always been fond of the bottle, unfortunately also being one of those people who become mean and belligerent when they've had one too many. No doubt, it had also affected his relations with the ABBA members back in the day.

With the sale of his companies, Stig didn't have very much to do with his time, and life no longer seemed to hold many interesting challenges for this always forward-moving man. For a few years he'd stayed on within the Sweden Music/Polar Music organization, acting as a consultant in putting together compilation CDs and such. But his drinking had only got worse and by the mid-1990s he didn't feel like doing much except sit at his kitchen table and drink Long John whisky and club soda.

Stig had used part of the funds received when he sold his companies to establish the Polar Music Prize. The prize is usually awarded to two different recipients each year, mostly shared by a popular music composer and someone working within the classical field. In its first year, 1992, one million was awarded to Paul McCartney while the three Baltic states (Lithuania, Latvia, and Estonia received one million kronor to

> ❝ The last few years have been tough. Stig was so ill and lost the will to live . . . I feel it was good for him that his life ended. He didn't enjoy anything anymore. ❞
>
> Gudrun Anderson

establish performing rights organizations. The Polar Music Prize's annual awards ceremony was about the only time that Stig was seen in public in the 1990s.

On the morning of September 12, 1997, Stig was at home, with only the cleaning lady for company; Gudrun was abroad on a holiday. Suddenly, he suffered a heart attack and collapsed. The cleaning lady called his daughter, Marie, whose offices were located nearby. She rushed over, but it was too late: The doctors later said that Stig had been gone even before he hit the floor. He was sixty-six years old.

Björn, Benny, and Frida attended the funeral, while Agnetha sent a wreath. Whatever one's feelings about this controversial man, one couldn't help being affected by the way the end came to someone who had been so successful in making Swedish popular music heard all over the world. "The last few years have been tough," said Gudrun a while later. "Stig was so ill and lost the will to live . . . I feel it was good for him that his life ended. He didn't enjoy anything anymore."

OPPOSITE Stig and Gudrun Anderson, 1990

ABBA GOLD— GREATEST HITS

TRACK LIST

Dancing Queen
Knowing Me, Knowing You
Take a Chance on Me
Mamma Mia
Lay All Your Love on Me
Super Trouper
I Have a Dream
The Winner Takes It All
Money, Money, Money
SOS
Chiquitita
Fernando
Voulez-Vous
Gimme! Gimme! Gimme!
  (A Man after Midnight)
Does Your Mother Know
One of Us
The Name of the Game
Thank You for the Music
Waterloo

Cover art:
Icon: layout

Released: September 21, 1992 (UK release date: September 21, 1992; US release date: September 21, 1993)

Label: Polydor 517 007-2

Notes

To accommodate the limited playing time on CDs at the time, the promotional edit of "The Name of the Game," also featured on *The Singles—The First Ten Years*, and an edited version of "Voulez-Vous"' were included on *ABBA Gold*. Later editions of the CD have reinstated the proper versions. "Thank You for the Music" was never really a global hit single, but was still included in lieu of proper hits such as "Ring Ring," "I Do, I Do, I Do, I Do, I Do," and "Summer Night City."

MORE ABBA GOLD— MORE ABBA HITS

MORE

ABBA®

GOLD

MORE ABBA HITS

TRACK LIST

Summer Night City
Angeleyes
The Day Before You Came
Eagle (single edit)
I Do, I Do, I Do, I Do, I Do
So Long
Honey, Honey
The Visitors
Our Last Summer
On and On and On
Ring Ring
I Wonder (Departure)
Lovelight
Head over Heels
When I Kissed the Teacher
I Am the City
Cassandra
Under Attack
When All Is Said and Done
The Way Old Friends Do

Cover art:
Icon: layout
Released: May 24, 1993 (UK release date: May 24, 1993; US release date: 1994)
Label: Polydor 519 353-2

Notes
This album featured the remainder of ABBA's international singles that hadn't been included on *ABBA Gold*: "Ring Ring," "Honey, Honey," "I Do, I Do, I Do, I Do, I Do," "Summer Night City," "Angeleyes" (a double A-side with "Voulez-Vous" in some countries), "Head over Heels," "The Day Before You Came," and "Under Attack." The version of "The Visitors" was a promotional edit, and "Eagle" was presented in its single edit, originally issued in 1978.

13

THREE MEN
AND A WEDDING

Three Men And A Wedding

The phenomenon known as jukebox musicals— creating an original work on the basis of songs that have already been made public—is not a new phenomenon. For example, old Hollywood musicals such as *Singin' in the Rain* were constructed around tunes that had been around for decades. But no jukebox musical has ever been as successful as *Mamma Mia!*

Producer Judy Craymer was a long-time friend of Björn and Benny, having been Tim Rice's assistant in the early 1980s and working closely with the trio that put together *Chess*. Since then she'd had the idea that it should be possible to do something with the ABBA songs. Björn and Benny were skeptical but told her that if she came up with something worthwhile, they would listen to her suggestion. By the mid-1990s, at least Björn was warming to the idea. In an almost childish way, as he admitted, he was missing the days of *Chess*, when he had a show to "look after" in London's West End. "I said to myself: 'Why don't I have a show here; other people have shows here. I should have one, too.'"

There was a breakthrough when writer Catherine Johnson finally came up with a viable story that could link together the ABBA songs in a reasonably credible manner. Her plot centers on a wedding of a young couple that is due to take place on a Greek island. The bride doesn't know who her father is, only that it could be one of three men. She invites them all to the wedding, much to the consternation of her mother, who has to confront events that took place two decades

PAGE 206 *Mamma Mia!*, 2008. (L-R) Christine Baranski, Meryl Streep, Julie Walters

OPPOSITE Björn and Frida attend the movie world premiere of *Mamma Mia!*, Odeon Leicester Square, June 30, 2008, London, UK

> **"In the beginning of our career the songs were more innocent and naïve, towards the end they were more mature . . . Therein lay the opening for a story about a mother and a daughter."**
>
> Björn

earlier. The key that made the whole thing work was how the earlier ABBA songs contrasted with their later work. "In the beginning of our career the songs were more innocent and naïve, towards the end they were more mature," said Björn. "And it was women who sang them. Therein lay the opening for a story about a mother and a daughter."

Opening at the Prince Edward Theatre—the same venue where *Chess* was originally staged— on April 6, 1999, it was twenty-five years to the day since ABBA had won the Eurovision Song Contest with "Waterloo." Those involved maintained that the date had been chosen purely to accommodate the schedule of director Phyllida Lloyd, but whether it was a coincidence or not, it was a marketer's dream. Björn took a deep breath and promoted both the show and ABBA's 25th anniversary anywhere and everywhere possible; the more media-shy Benny said that Björn ought to be given an award for all the interviews he had given. Indeed, Benny remained doubtful about the show's prospects until the opening night, when the audience's rapturous reception of this feel-good production proved him wrong. Recalled Judy Craymer, "[Benny] turned to me and said, 'You can say it now.' I flashed back, 'I told you so!'"

As a result of the attention bestowed on the musical and the group that had once originated the songs featured in it, the ABBA revival—which some had surmised would be a very temporary phenomenon, going on for a year or two—reached new heights. *ABBA Gold* returned to the No. 1 spot in the UK, and the musical was a hit beyond anything the production team had dared expect. Ever-cautious Björn had hoped that the show could run for a couple of years in the West End, but it's now been going for more than two decades. *Mamma Mia!* subsequently opened in local productions in almost every country on the planet, the New York production running for fourteen years, making it the ninth-longest-running show in the history of Broadway. In all its incarnations across the globe, the stage production has been seen by more than sixty million people.

In 2008, the musical was made into a blockbuster movie, starring Meryl Streep as Donna, the mother, Amanda Seyfried as Sophie, her daughter, and Pierce Brosnan, Colin Firth, and Stellan Skarsgård as the three possible fathers. Again, the commercial success exceeded anyone's wildest dreams. *Mamma Mia! The Movie* was the fifth-highest-grossing film of 2008, and placed high on all sorts of all-time-achievement lists. The less than stellar singing by some of the actors—not least Pierce Brosnan, whose voice, variously described as "a water buffalo" or "a wounded raccoon," became something of a running joke—did nothing to hurt the film's runaway success. In 2018, a sequel, *Mamma Mia! Here We Go Again*, reunited the original cast, added a host of additional stars to the lineup, including Cher and Andy Garcia, and was also a huge hit.

Mamma Mia! in all its incarnations, along with a gradual re-evaluation of ABBA's place in the history of popular music, somehow interacted to cement their status, making them a reference point in all

OPPOSITE Benny (R) onstage with the cast of the musical *Mamma Mia!*, on its opening night in 1999

RIGHT Movie posters for *Mamma Mia!* (2008) and *Mamma Mia! Here We Go Again* (2018)

BELOW *Mamma Mia! Here We Go Again*. (L-R) Jessica Keenan Wynn, Lily James, Alexa Davies

sorts of cultural contexts. Consequently, if Agnetha, Björn, Benny, and Frida had ever thought that they could escape their identities as ex-ABBA members in the public imagination, they had to accept that this was never going to happen. At the start of the new millennium, Benny, whose ethos was always to move forward with his music, admitted that he was proud and happy of ABBA's revival, but also expressed concern that it was a "sign of poverty" when "the greatest success is generated by something that was made 20 years ago." But with the explosive triumph of *Mamma Mia!*, even he had to concede that he had no choice but to "throw in the towel" and accept that ABBA and its legacy would always overshadow whatever else he was trying to achieve as a musician. Together with Frida, he even went to New York City to attend ABBA's induction into the Rock and Roll Hall of Fame in 2010, the induction itself being unthinkable a decade or two earlier.

For Agnetha, who was still shunning the limelight as best she could, the new millennium got off to a less than pleasurable start. In the late 1990s she had entered into a relationship with a Dutch ABBA fan named Gert van der Graaf. He had long been obsessed with Agnetha, even going so far as to purchase a house near her farm estate on the island of Ekerö outside Stockholm. Despite these warning signs, Agnetha still gave in to his courting and they became a couple. After a while, though, she realized that the relationship wasn't viable and broke it off in September 1999. Van der Graaf refused to accept her decision and began stalking her, sending eighty-six letters over the course of five months, and showing up regularly outside her house. Agnetha eventually reported him to the police and the case went to court. As a result of the trial that followed, a restraining order was filed and van der Graaf was ordered to leave the country.

Even before this sad story, Agnetha had been

labeled a "recluse" by the press, conjuring up images of a Greta Garbo "wanting to be alone" or perhaps a female version of Howard Hughes, cooped up on her farm, refusing to see anyone. The truth was that she was leading a fairly normal life, as "normal" as it could be for a financially independent woman. She spent her time taking care of the horses and dogs on her farm, seeing her grandchildren, meeting up with friends, going to parties, sometimes being spotted shopping in central Stockholm. It was just that she wasn't interested in leading a life in the public eye. She admitted that, following the end of her recording career, she had grown tired of music and had become sensitive to noise; maybe, like Frida, she also needed time to put herself together again after the intense ABBA period.

But she also maintained that she hadn't closed any doors, and in 2004 she surprised everyone by returning to the recording studio and releasing a brand-new album; Agnetha explained that the main impetus had been the many letters she received from fans wanting to hear her voice again. *My Colouring Book*, a well-produced collection of covers, mainly of songs she had liked in her youth, hit No. 1 in Sweden, reached the Top Ten in some countries, and peaked at No. 12 in the UK, a better result than any of her previous solo efforts. Promotion was limited as ever: A TV special was put together and a select few interviews with print media were conducted, but that was all.

Agnetha later admitted that she thought this would be her last album, but in 2011 she was approached by producer and songwriter Jörgen Elofsson, part of the growing wave of successful hitmakers Sweden had produced since the 1990s; his past work included songs for Britney Spears, Westlife, and Kelly Clarkson, among others. Elofsson and his arranger-partner Peter Nordahl had a bunch of songs they thought could be suitable for Agnetha. A meeting was arranged and her

reaction was very favorable indeed. "I just couldn't say 'no,'" she recalled. "I really loved the songs from the beginning." A modern-sounding hit album, simply entitled *A*, was issued in May 2013, becoming her most successful solo release, hitting the Top Ten in more than ten countries. Notably, the album featured her first new songwriting effort in almost thirty years, "I Keep Them on the Floor beside My Bed," with lyrics by Jörgen Elofsson, a compelling ballad harking back to her mid-1970s songwriting style.

No doubt, part of the album's success was due to the fact that she had done more promotion than at any time since the ABBA days. She started out by receiving plenty of media in Stockholm, then, surprisingly, agreed to spend ten days in London, doing a number of television and radio interviews. Her sudden availability startled those who'd bought into the "eccentric reclusive"

label. Once the promotion was over, though, she again largely disappeared from public view, being seen at the occasional party or premiere over the years, but not making herself available for interviews. Not living the life of a recluse, exactly, but trying to be as normal as she could be as the ex-member of one of the world's most legendary bands.

ABOVE LEFT Agnetha comes to London to promote *A*; her first album in nine years, 2013

ABOVE RIGHT Agnetha receives a Gold Award for sales of *A* at the Pride festival in Stockholm, Sweden, August 2013

OPPOSITE Frida rehearses with British musician Jon Lord of Deep Purple (L) ahead of the José Carreras Gala in Leipzig, Germany, 2004

Frida, meanwhile, had gone through her own share of tragedies as the 1990s were edging toward the 2000s. In 1998, her daughter, Lise-Lotte, died in an accident, while the following year her husband, Ruzzo, passed away from cancer. There had been talk of a follow-up album to her 1996 release, *Djupa andetag*, but all such plans were cancelled as, once again, she found she had to find a new life for herself. She didn't stop singing completely, but she only appeared as a guest vocalist on mostly rather obscure releases by friends and acquaintances. The most high-profile of these was the song "The Sun Will Shine Again," featured on a 2004 album by former Deep Purple keyboardist Jon Lord. Frida even agreed to promote the song by performing it on German TV, and also at one of Lord's concerts. The song's lyrics, about finding a light at the end of the tunnel after going through

rough times, resonated with her personal experience of the last few years. "[When you're] in the kind of void where it's really dark and you really don't know how to climb out of it again," she said, "then suddenly you see the light above you and you know that this is really true, that the sun will shine on you again."

But not long after the release of the Jon Lord album, Frida made clear that she wasn't about to stage a full-scale comeback. "The motivation regarding my musical career doesn't exist anymore," she said. "It was there for a long time, perhaps up until a few years ago, but there is a time for everything and that time has now passed. There are so many other things that I'd like to devote myself to that perhaps haven't got so much to do with music." She found a new companion in Henry Smith, an heir to the fortune generated by the WH Smith chain of retail stores, the couple dividing

> **❝ The motivation regarding my musical career doesn't exist anymore . . . there is a time for everything and that time has now passed. ❞**
>
> Frida

LEFT Frida and partner, Henry Smith arrive to the premiere of the theatrical dining experience, *Mamma Mia The Party* at the Tyrol restaurant in Stockholm, Sweden, January 20, 2016

OPPOSITE Benny with poet Kristina Lugn, at the Orion Theatre in Stockholm, Sweden, 2012

their time between Switzerland, Sweden, Majorca, and England. It became an essentially private life, with little of the couple being heard or seen, except when Frida attended a *Mamma Mia!* opening or the occasional ABBA-related event.

After the major undertaking that was the *Kristina från Duvemåla* musical, it was almost as if Björn and Benny couldn't quite face doing anything similar again. There was constant talk of writing another musical, and suggestions as to what it would be about, but the discussions somehow never amounted to anything. For Benny's part, his regular music outlet instead became Benny Anderssons orkester, known outside Sweden as the Benny Andersson Band. Issuing their first album in 2001, the band—featuring Benny on keyboards and accordion—largely records and performs music harking back to Swedish folk roots and to the kind of hits that were popular between the 1930s and 1950s. With *Kristina* star Helen Sjöholm and *Chess* star Tommy

Körberg as its featured vocalists, the band has issued a number of successful albums since 2001, also conducting equally successful summer tours of Sweden. Benny has otherwise written music for films, also contributing commissioned pieces for inaugurations and celebrations of prestigious events. In 2017, he issued an album entitled *Piano*, featuring instrumental solo renditions of tunes he'd written or co-written over the years, from the ABBA period up to the present. ABBA were not represented by any of their most familiar classics, Benny instead opting for album tracks in the vein of *Arrival*'s "My Love, My Life" or should-have-been-hits such as "The Day Before You Came."

Tellingly, when Björn and Benny finally wrote a musical again, it was only because they'd been approached with an offer to become part of a project not instigated by them. *Hjälp sökes* ("Help Wanted") was a small-scale, somewhat bizarre production—there were live animals onstage, including cows—that opened at one of Stockholm's more modest theaters in 2013. Björn wasn't even meant to be involved, but was drafted in when the book writer—poet, playwright, and Swedish Academy member Kristina Lugn—realized that she wasn't up to the task of writing the lyrics. Within its limitations, the show was a success, attracting rave reviews. Benny's music was pretty much of the tasteful variety you'd come to expect of him, while Björn's lyrics were more surprising, as he'd been forced to step out of his rather polished universe and into the quirky world of Kristina Lugn.

For Björn, the creation of music is rather a sideline in the twenty-first century. He writes lyrics, mainly for Benny, when requested, but otherwise much of his time is devoted to various entrepreneurial projects, mainly within the world of real estate. He has been involved in everything from building a residential/hotel complex in his hometown of Västervik, to converting a former office block in Stockholm to apartments for young adults. More surprisingly, given ABBA's reluctance to discuss politics and such in their heyday, Björn has also emerged as a voice advocating for or against a range of issues, writing opinion pieces on everything

from religion and euthanasia to the possibilities of a cash-free society. He has also become a spokesman for a fairer distribution of royalties for artists and performers on music streaming platforms such as Spotify: Although he himself, as an ABBA member, benefits from the current system, he insists that it's unfair to those who aren't fortunate enough to be as big as ABBA.

A dedicated jogger in the ABBA days, even running a number of marathons, he eventually gave up on this, slipping into a less healthy lifestyle. A lover of fine wines, he finally admitted to himself that he was an alcoholic and stopped drinking sometime around 2007 to 2008. "It affected my life too much," he said, adding that giving up alcohol was "the best decision I've ever made." His songwriting partner had similar problems and decided to face the music even earlier than Björn, giving up drinking in the early part of the new millennium. "If you realise that you don't feel like yourself unless you have alcohol in your body, then it's time to quit," Benny said. "I thought, 'I have a fantastic life, a fantastic family, and everything is going well.

Should all that be thrown away just because I'm unable to stop drinking alcohol?'"

Among Björn's entrepreneurial projects in the second decade of the twenty-first century was the foundation of ABBA The Museum in Stockholm. Originally a project instigated by people outside the ABBA organization, Björn eventually decided that he wanted to take a greater part in it, becoming the main investor and promoting it as much as he possibly could. Opening in May 2013, ABBA The Museum was an instant success and is in the top ten of the Stockholm tourist board's *Things to do in Stockholm* list. Apart from Elvis Presley's Graceland and The Beatles Story in Liverpool, not many museums devoted to musical artists have achieved such long-term success.

With the continued presence of ABBA, the inevitable question in interviews became: Are you ever going to get back together? After all, almost every legendary band of the 1960s to 1980s era had done it. Whatever tension there may have been between the four members in the years immediately following their split,

it was long gone by now, so why not get back together again? The answer was simple: They just didn't feel like it. Not because of any animosity between them, but because it would mean going back to something that had been and gone. "Pop music is for the young and we have passed that stage in our lives," explained Björn. Not even an offer of a mind-blowing $1 billion, in exchange for an extensive world tour and a new album, was enough to tempt them. Björn pointed to a comment made by Led Zeppelin's Robert Plant who quipped, when that band reformed temporarily, that they had become their own covers band. Not even raising money for charity would be motivation enough. No, determined Björn in the many interviews where the question of ABBA's reunion came up, if it were ever to happen, it would have to be for another reason entirely—the right reason. ABBA would remain, again in Björn's words, "the group that never came back."

OPPOSITE ABBA The Museum in Stockholm, Sweden
BELOW Inside ABBA The Museum on the eve of its official opening in May 2013

14

ON A
VOYAGE

On A Voyage

Back in late 1977 and early 1978, when ABBA simultaneously launched *ABBA–The Album* and *ABBA–The Movie*, the co-ordination of both campaigns was regarded as the height of clever blanket marketing. Sporting similar artwork, the brief from Stig Anderson to art director Rune Söderqvist was that the film should sell the album and the album should sell the film. In Sweden, Stig had also ensured that upon release day, the album was available everywhere: not just in your regular record stores, but at department stores, gas stations and convenience stores.

The campaigns afforded that album and movie, as far-reaching as they seemed at the time, will nevertheless pale in comparison with the meticulously planned and executed promotion of ABBA's 2021 comeback album *Voyage,* and the digital live concert experience entitled *ABBA Voyage*. Starting on August 26, with cryptic hints across social media and the appearance of billboards in various cities around the world, everything culminated on September 2, when a live press conference featuring Björn and Benny announced that not only would ABBA release a couple of new songs and produce a digital avatar live experience–which had been known for a few years–but they would also, against all odds, issue a brand new studio album. The announcement became front page news across the globe, exploded on social media– "breaking the internet" to use current vernacular–and even BBC Radio postponed its otherwise immovable six o'clock news so that it could play "I Still Have Faith in You," one of the brand new ABBA songs, which was unveiled to the world at that precise hour.

But how did the extraordinary, completely unexpected recording of an album come about in the first place? After all, from comments made by all members of the group during the thirty-nine years that had passed since ABBA's final recording sessions, it was made abundantly clear that hell would have to freeze over not once but perhaps ten times before a reunion could happen. Occasional, non-committal statements had been made in interviews, along the lines of, "well, one should never say never," but as far as the outside world knew, there had never been any actual, serious discussions about it.

The catalyst behind the ABBA reunion was rather surprising: Simon Fuller, former manager of the Spice Girls, and the creator of television formats such as *Idol* in all its international variations. In 2016, it was revealed that he had approached ABBA with a suggestion: What if you could tour live as digital versions of yourself, using the latest cutting-edge technology? Fuller explained that it would be much more advanced than what had been seen so far, in the shape of holograms of deceased artists such as Michael Jackson and Tupac Shakur. In effect, the ABBA members would be able to "go on the road without going on the road," as Benny phrased it. "We could remain at home, cooking dinner or walking the dog. We thought, 'Huh? Well, that's actually an interesting idea.'" ABBA felt that it was worth trying, primarily, they said, because as far as the technology was concerned, it hadn't been done before.

The tour would feature the ABBA members as they looked in their heyday, the repertoire encompassing most of their classic hits plus perhaps a number of album tracks. And here lay the opening for a more tangible reunion, one that would move beyond the merely digital and involve the four flesh-and-blood

PAGE 220 People watch the ABBA *Voyage* event, at which ABBA announce a new album, Gröna Lund amusement park, Stockholm, Sweden, September 2, 2021
OPPOSITE At the ABBA *Voyage* event in Berlin, Germany, September 2, 2021

members themselves. Explained Benny a few years later, "We said, 'If we'd done this for real, gone on tour as 75-year-olds and put on a show, we would have had at least two new songs'. So I called Agnetha and Frida and said, 'Ehm... what do you say? Would you like to record two new songs?' And they said, 'Yes!' It surprised me a bit [because] ABBA just hasn't been on the table–not for anyone of us: not for me and not for them either. Agnetha has tried to keep away from being an ABBA member. Me as well–I want to be me, not an 'ABBA.'"

By May 2017, two new songs had been written, and Benny got together with his favorite session musicians to lay down the instrumental backing track. The following month, and much to their own surprise, ABBA found themselves together in a recording studio–Benny's own RMV Studios, which he and his son Ludvig opened in 2011–recording vocals for new ABBA songs for the first time in thirty-five years. As Agnetha would recall, she "had no idea what to expect," and no doubt her band members shared that feeling, although Benny later related that his concerns were of a more practical nature: just minutes before Agnetha and Frida came to the studio, he realized that

he hadn't really asked them if they could still sing. It turned out they could–their voices sounded different, a little lower, a little older, perhaps even a little frailer here and there, but with the personality, energy and capacity for interpretation intact.

Whatever other apprehension may have colored the atmosphere in that studio, it vanished quickly as the four members entered into a kind of time-warp. "It just took moments," remembered Björn. "We were kind of looking at each other and then [we went] straight back, like no time had passed at all. It was amazing." He put it down to the friendship that they'd been able to maintain over the decades once the dust had settled after the painful divorces. "There are such strong bonds between us," he said, "because of all these wonderful, mind-boggling experiences we've gone through together."

Incredibly, the explosive news that one of the world's most legendary pop groups had created new

ABOVE A new ABBA album and a hologram show is announced in front of fans in Berlin, Germany

OPPOSITE Benny, Stockholm, Sweden, October 20, 2021

> **66 There are such strong bonds between us, because of all these wonderful, mind-boggling experiences we've gone through together. 99**
>
> Björn

music was kept secret from the general public until almost a year later. But on April 27, 2018, there was finally an announcement, although ABBA themselves would have preferred to keep things under wraps a while longer. Their hand was forced, however, by an ABBA television special to be co-produced by NBC in the US and the BBC in the UK, scheduled to air in December 2018. One of the new songs was to be unveiled in the television special, which was centered around big name artists performing their own versions of ABBA songs. A music video for a ballad entitled "I Still Have Faith in You" featuring the new avatars would be the cherry on the cake, and since NBC wanted to start promoting the upcoming broadcast, ABBA had to announce the new songs in order to "own" that part of the news.

Needless to say, the announcement was all over the media–social and mainstream–within seconds of being made public, and for many outlets it was among the biggest stories of the day. There wasn't much information about the actual songs, but the world learned that one of them was "I Still Have Faith in You" and that the other was the up-tempo "Don't Shut Me Down."

So far, so good–but controlling the narrative of how the songs would be unveiled to the world began to go wrong soon afterwards. The television special was suddenly postponed and, before long, cancelled altogether, while a series of proposed release dates for the new songs came and went. "I'm not saying when anymore," a presumably frustrated Björn stated in an interview. "I'm just saying we have them and they will be released eventually." It now seemed like no one was really in control, and that it would be anybody's

LEFT Björn in Benny's studio on Skeppsholmen in Stockholm, Sweden, October 20, 2021

Benny's youngest son, Ludvig, who had taken on the role of overall producer. The show would be directed by Baillie Walsh, known for a number of top-client commercials as well as music videos and feature films.

However, at some point Simon Fuller and the tech company that he had brought on board left the project, reportedly because Fuller and his team hadn't quite been able to deliver avatars that were up to the standard they had promised. Instead, the Industrial Light & Magic company (ILM)–founded by *Star Wars* creator, George Lucas and renowned for being at the forefront of visual effects–stepped in, upping the game considerably.

It became clear that if the avatars were to work as well as everyone hoped, then the technological set-up would be so complex that to take them on tour would not be viable. Rather, the show would need to be performed at one fixed venue, and not your regular concert hall or arena either, due to technical specifications that had to be considered. Benny remembered how he and Björn were in London for meetings about the project when Benny came up with a suggestion. "I said to Björn, 'Why don't we do it here?' 'Well, there's no arena,' he said." And then–in the almost flippant way unique to those who are both kronor billionaires and safe in the knowledge that there would be plenty of investors queuing up to be part of the venture–Benny offered an extravagant solution to the problem: they could build an arena themselves. London, they both agreed, would be the perfect city because of its status as the entertainment capital of Europe. The site chosen for the ABBA Arena, as it was christened, was the Queen Elizabeth Olympic Park.

As if ABBA reuniting in the recording studio wasn't extraordinary enough, in early 2020 the four members donned black motion capture costumes with colored dots on them, looking for all the world as extras in some science fiction adventure, spending five weeks in a Stockholm studio to give ILM what they needed to construct the avatars: accurate images of their actual movements and stage mannerisms.

While Agnetha later related how the recording of the new songs had been fairly easy to say yes to, she had hesitated slightly at the prospect of performing eight hours a day for five consecutive weeks. No doubt, the other three members of ABBA were also less than enthusiastic about that prospect, although they all overcame it. It seems the greatest hurdle for Björn and Benny was that in order to capture their facial movements properly, they had to shave off their beards completely–Benny hadn't been seen without

guess if and when the world would ever hear the songs and see the much-touted avatars. The narrative had changed from "the exciting new ABBA songs" to "the delayed new ABBA songs."

Meanwhile, rumors were rampant as to exactly how many songs had been recorded. Throughout 2019, there were unconfirmed reports that a total of three songs were in the can, the number eventually jumping to five. While long-time ABBA watchers remained skeptical, yet hopeful, by the time of the 2021 *Voyage* launch, Benny revealed that the rumors had actually been true. "When we had [the first] two songs it felt a little thin–'shouldn't we do a few more?',", he explained, the thinking being that instead of just one or two singles, they could at least release an EP. "So, we did a few more and they turned out good."

ABBA may have been busy in the recording studio, but those working on the avatars were perhaps even busier. Producer Svana Gisla and co-executive producer and director Johan Renck–the team behind David Bowie's final videos–were on board, as was

RIGHT Frida, attends the wedding of John Ledin and Countess Alexandra Hamilton, Kristianstad, Sweden, 2018
OPPOSITE Agnetha, 2016

one for fifty years, Björn for almost forty. Producer Svana Gisla remembered how they'd looked at her in "utter bewilderment and said: 'That's absolutely not going to happen.' I looked over at the 180 people with computer monitors and said: 'I am sorry Benny but you are going to have to shave or I will have to send everyone home.'" ABBA's songwriting team had no choice but to bring out the razors.

The timing of the filming was fortunate. Just prior to everyone getting together in Stockholm, there had been increasingly worrying reports of a virus spreading rapidly in China and beyond. By March 2020, when the ABBA filming was already over, the Covid-19 pandemic was a fact, shutting down most activities that involved a large number of people being together in the same room.

The rumors on exactly how many new tracks had been recorded by ABBA continued unabated. As would finally be revealed in September 2021, the four members had enjoyed the experience of being together in the studio for the second time just as much as the first, to the extent that the suggestion of a recording a further few songs came up–in fact, completing an entire album. It was almost incomprehensible that what had only a few years earlier been dismissed as something that was highly unlikely to happen, could now take place as if the members had thought it over for a few seconds and then simply decided to go ahead with it. Just like that. The recording sessions for the remaining songs took place in 2021.

Finally released on November 5, 2021, *Voyage* had been preceded by the two previously announced singles, both issued on September 2. The stately and pensive ballad "I Still Have Faith in You," with Frida on lead vocals, was a reflection on ABBA themselves–their history, their legacy and their reunion, lyricist Björn commenting that once he heard the tune that Benny sent to him, he realized that the lyrics "had to be about us." As such, this statement of intent signaled that it should be the first song unleashed on the world.

If musically "I Still Have Faith in You" mirrored how Benny Andersson's music sounded in the twenty-first century, the second song, the Agnetha-led "Don't Shut Me Down," was a surprising throwback to ABBA's glorious mid-to-late-1970s period. Benny revealed that he had been watching the 2015 television series *River*,

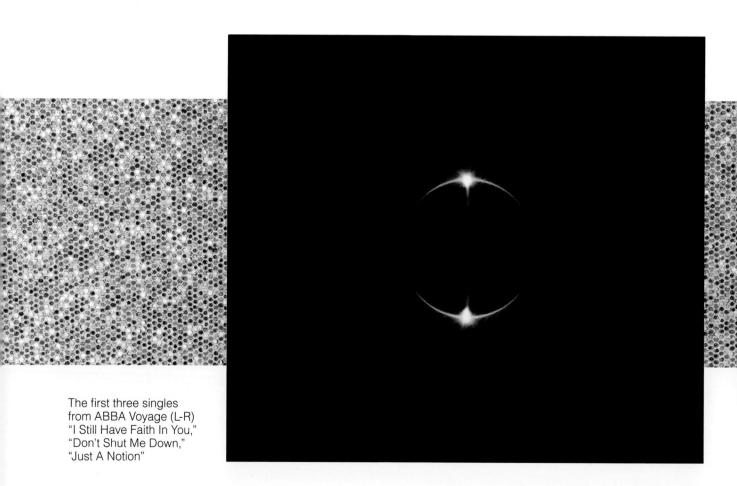

The first three singles from ABBA Voyage (L-R) "I Still Have Faith In You," "Don't Shut Me Down," "Just A Notion"

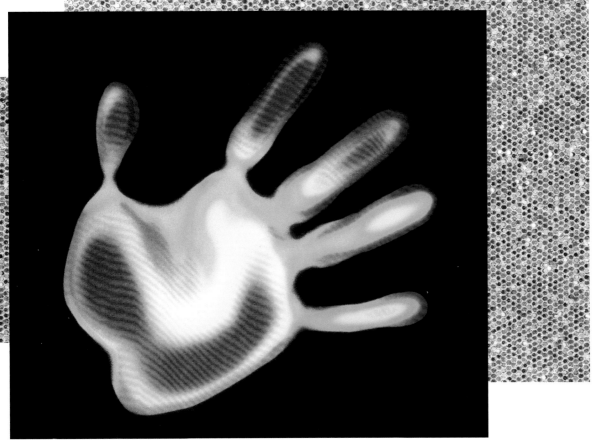

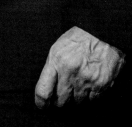

British radio presenter Zoe Ball poses with Björn (L) and Benny (R) during the London launch of ABBA *Voyage*, September 2, 2021, UK

LEFT The new ABBA album *Voyage* on display at a local record store in Stockholm on November 4, 2021, ahead of the official release on November 5, 2021

PAGES 238–239 ABBA give the thumbs up after winning the Eurovision Song Contest with their song "Waterloo." (L-R) Björn Ulvaeus, Agnetha Fältskog, Anni-Frid "Frida" Lyngstad and Benny Andersson.

starring Stellan Skarsgård and Nicola Walker, where Tina Charles's 1976 hit "I Love to Love" is featured, triggering the idea that one of the new ABBA songs should be in that vein; Benny's demo title for the tune was even "Tina Charles." By far the more popular of the two songs, hitting number one in Sweden and Switzerland, this jubilant number bore all the hallmarks of classic ABBA: the super-sharp, magic and sorely missed vocal harmonies that only Agnetha and Frida could conjure up, and a mass of keyboard overdub and flourishes from Benny, with plenty of affectionate nods to hits of yore such as "Dancing Queen."

The remainder of the album didn't feature any tunes that harked back to ABBA's heyday in the same obvious way, but was nevertheless a highly satisfying collection of songs. Agnetha and Frida both sounded older, which was to be expected, but not necessarily in a way that diminished the attraction of their voices; rather, their aging showcased new qualities. On the 1980s-style rock number "No Doubt About It," for instance, the benefit of experience works in Frida's favor: she probably couldn't have delivered such an astounding lead vocal in quite the same convincing way forty years earlier.

Musically, the album was varied, and the lyrics offered new spins on familiar ABBA themes such as divorces: only ABBA could make a dance track out of the handing over of a child from one divorced parent to the other, as they do in the Agnetha-sung "Keep an Eye on Dan." Elsewhere, in the country-ballad "I Can

Be That Woman," also with Agnetha on lead vocals, they introduced completely new relationship themes, such as a marriage marred by one of the parties being a little too fond of the bottle (was Björn in some way inspired by his and Benny's own experiences as alcoholics?). Benny brought out his old synthesizers from the ABBA days–primarily the Minimoog and the Yamaha GX-1, the latter of which had dominated the soundscape on ABBA's two final studio albums–and, while largely producing the album in accordance with his modern day tastes and aesthetics, threw in references to classic ABBA here and there.

Voyage received mixed reviews, some scribes praising it to the skies, while others–perhaps mainly those who had expected a return to the sounds and styles of "Dancing Queen" and "The Winner Takes It All"–found it a resounding disappointment. The overall reception was positive, however, and in terms of sales the album was a success long before it was issued. In combination with the skilful promotional campaign and an impressive number of media interviews conducted by Björn and Benny, it was almost a foregone conclusion that the album would enter the charts at No. 1 in a mind-blowing eighteen countries, selling more than one million copies in its first week. *Voyage* even hit No. 2 in the United States, by far ABBA's most impressive album chart position in that part of the world; *ABBA–The Album* having hit No.14 in 1978.

In all, *Voyage* constituted a comeback that was both dignified and successful: ABBA had been absolutely right to still have faith in themselves. But was it the start of a new, well, voyage, for the group or was this the end of the story? Benny made it clear in an interview that although he had never previously said that ABBA would never do anything together again, this time, after *Voyage*, he felt prepared to state that this was the end of the line. Agnetha made similar comments: only Frida offered a "never say never" perspective. With three quarters of the group now in their mid-seventies, it does seem likely they will want to regard *Voyage* as a more satisfying end to their story than their early 1980s fizzling out, rather than the start of a new chapter.

Monumental as the comeback was in itself, the recording of ABBA's new music was like a hobby project in comparison with the number of people involved in the digital avatar project, *ABBA Voyage*. About 850 people have been engaged in putting it all together, including a ten-piece band that perform live alongside the digital ABBA members. The man in charge of assembling the musicians was James Righton, formerly a member of Klaxons, a British band

that scored great domestic success with their 2007 debut album *Myths Of The Near Future*. Among the ABBA band members is British singer Little Boots, herself a successful recording artist who hit the UK Top Ten with her 2009 debut album. The production team wanted the real live people onstage to be performers in themselves, and able to project a sense of flesh-and-blood excitement to the audience.

As intriguing and groundbreaking as this hi-tech cross between a theme park and a live concert was, its main importance may very well be that it achieved the almost-impossible and brought ABBA back together in the studio again. Their return meant a lot to their millions of fans across the globe, but the recording of the album had also been a source of joy to the four members. Björn spoke of "a feeling of gratitude to be in this situation again, to be creative together with [the other ABBA members]. It felt marvellous."

"Those first sessions back in 2018 were such fun," stated Frida in a press release, "and when Benny called and asked if I'd consider singing some more I jumped at it! And what songs!! My respect and love go out to these exceptionally talented, truly genius songwriters! Such joy it was to work with the group again. I am so happy with what we have made." Agnetha, ever-cautious each time she was asked to re-enter the world of showbusiness, said that when she first arrived at Benny's studio, she found it "such a friendly and safe environment" that everything became enjoyable within minutes. She also reflected on the hesitation over whether her and Frida's voices would hold up four decades after their last recordings together. "We heard pretty immediately–from both Frida's voice and mine–that it sounded more or less as it did back then. But you may have to make another kind of effort and give more of your ability to tell a story, to empathise with the song. I always used to do that, but it's a lot more now that one has lived an entire life. You put more emotion into it."

It was Benny, though, who summed up what may have been the single most emotionally resonant aspect of ABBA's return, both for their fans and for the group itself. While he acknowledged that creating the concert experience had been joyful enough, the reunion in the recording studio was probably even more powerful. As he phrased it, "I think hearing Frida and Agnetha singing again is hard to beat."

VOYAGE

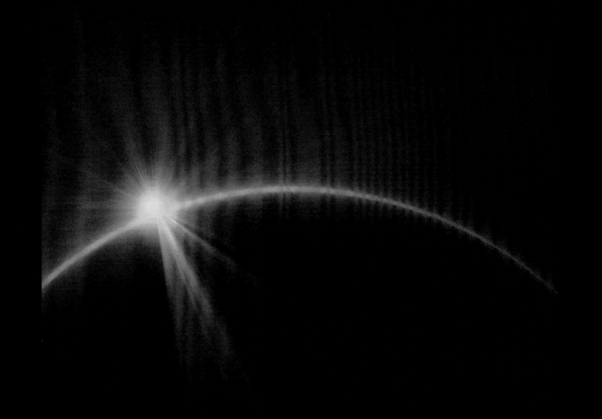

ABBA Voyage

TRACK LIST

I Still Have Faith in You
When You Danced with Me
Little Things
Don't Shut Me Down
Just a Notion
I Can Be That Woman
Keep an Eye on Dan
Bumble Bee
No Doubt About It
Ode to Freedom

Recorded: RMV Studios, ("Just a Notion" partially recorded at Polar Music Studio), mixed at Mono Music Studios, Stockholm, Sweden

Produced and arranged by: Benny Andersson

Assistant producer: Björn Ulvaeus

Engineering and ProTools programming by: Bernard Löhr

Assistant engineering: Linn Fijal and Vilma Colling

Engineering of original "Just a Notion" recording: Michael B. Tretow

Personnel:
Agnetha Fältskog: vocals
Anni-Frid Lyngstad: vocals
Björn Ulvaeus: vocals
Benny Andersson: vocals, keyboards
Lasse Wellander: guitar
Lasse Jonsson: guitar
Mats Englund: bass ("I Can Be That Woman")
Per Lindvall: drums and percussion
Pär Grebacken: recorder, clarinet and tenor saxophone
Jan Bengtson: flute and baritone saxophone
Stockholm Concert Orchestra: strings
Göran Arnberg: orchestration and conducting
Members from Children's Choir of Stockholm
    International School (SIS): vocals
Kimberley Akester, with assistance from Anneli
    Thompson: SIS choir direction

Cover art:
Baillie Walsh: design
Johan Renck: photography

Released: November 5, 2021 (UK release date: November 5, 2021; US release date: November 5, 2021)

Label: Polar 00602438614820

Notes
For the album, ABBA unearthed an unfinished recording dating back to the 1978 *Voulez-Vous* sessions, entitled "Just a Notion." This "Waterloo"-style song was stripped of its original backing, with only the vocals remaining intact from the 1978 version, and a brand new arrangement built around it.

ACKNOWLEDGMENTS

After researching and writing about ABBA for more than thirty years, my brain is chock-full of facts about the group's history, my findings having been shared in a number of books, the most well-known perhaps being *Bright Lights Dark Shadows—The Real Story Of ABBA* and *ABBA—The Complete Recording Sessions*. In a sense, then—and while acknowledging the books, journals, radio and television programmes that I have consulted over the years—I have somehow ended up being my own main source of information. Similarly, many of the quotes from ABBA members and others in their circle featured in *ABBA At 50* come from my own interviews, conducted 1993–2016. The present volume also features an interview quote from a 1998 interview with Benny Andersson by Dan-Eric Landén, with whom I co-wrote a book about the Hep Stars. Listed below are some of the other sources for interview quotes.

I would like to extend a warm thanks to my friend and fellow ABBA fan Ian Cole, who has read through and commented on virtually everything I've written in the English language for more than two decades, and also to everyone at Palazzo Editions who commissioned this book and have been so very easy to work with.

SOURCES

BOOKS

Andersson, Benny; Ulvaeus, Björn; and Craymer, Judy, *Mamma Mia! How Can I Resist You?*: Weidenfeld & Nicolson, 2006

Borg, Christer, *Fenomenet ABBA*: Sweden Music, 1977

Fältskog, Agnetha, *Som jag är. Livsbilder berättade för Brita Åhman*: Norstedts, Stockholm, 1996

Gradvall, Jan; Karlsson, Petter; Wanselius, Bengt; Wikström, Jeppe, *ABBA The Photo Book*: Bokförlaget Max Ström, 2014

Hedlund, Oscar, *Stikkan: den börsnoterade refrängsångaren*: Sweden Music, 1983

Karlsson, Petter, *Min pappa hette Stikkan*: Anderson Pocket, 2008

Schulman, Leif, and Hammarsten, Charles, *Succé på världs-scenen: Agnetha, Björn, Benny & Annifrid*: Allerbok, 1979

Waller, Johnny, *The Phil Collins Story*: Zomba, 1985

MAGAZINES, NEWSPAPERS AND PRESS RELEASES

ABBA Magazine/International ABBA Magazine, Aftonbladet, Allers, Clic, Dagens Industri, Dagens Nyheter, The Daily Express, The Daily Mirror, Dover Times Reporter, Expressen, The Guardian, Hi-Fi & Musik, Melody Maker, Min Värld, Mojo, News Of The World, The Observer, Songwriter, Svensk Damtidning, Swedish Press, Vecko-Revyn, Vi, Voyage press release

TV, DVD, RADIO AND WEBSITES

Avsminkat, Frida—The DVD, Livet är en fest, Mamma Mia! (mamma-mia.com), *MTV, PSL, Skavlan, Svensktoppen, Voyage EPK*

PICTURE CREDITS

T: Top; B: Bottom; L: Left; R: Right

ALAMY: P9, P59 Keystone Press/Alamy Stock Photo P12, P20, P21, P27, P42, P53, P179, P184, P197, P200 Roger Tillberg/Alamy Stock Photo P16 Bengt af Geijerstam/Bonnierarkivet/TT P19 Hans Jansson/SCANPIX P22, P24, P25, P26, P28T, P28B, P30, P32, P34, P37, P39, P43, P45, P62, P65, P68T, P94, P101, P107T, P142-143, P148, P150, P156, P180, P196, P216, P217, P226-227, P229 TT News Agency/Alamy Stock Photo P31, P36, P38, P138 Classic Picture Library/Alamy Stock Photo P57 Pictorial Press Ltd/Alamy Stock Photo P68B Album/Alamy Stock Photo P134, P139 Trinity Mirror/Mirrorpix/Alamy Stock Photo P152, P195 Collection Christophel/Alamy Stock Photo P164T René van den Berg/Alamy Stock Photo P165, P222, P224 dpa picture alliance/Alamy Stock Photo P176 INTERFOTO/Alamy Stock Photo P198 Sueddeutsche Zeitung Photo/Alamy Stock Photo P211TL Everett Collection Inc/Alamy Stock Photo P212 REUTERS/Alamy Stock Photo P214R WENN Rights Ltd/Alamy Stock Photo P218 Rolf_52/Alamy Stock Photo BBC: COVER Copyright © BBC Photo Library CAMERA PRESS: P48 Heilemann/Camera Press GETTY: P8 Photo by Michael Ochs Archives/Getty Images P10 Photo by Mike Prior/Redferns P11 Photo by Peter Bischoff/Getty Images P15, P18 Photo by Gunter Zint/K & K Ulf Kruger OHG/Redferns P41 Photo by GAB Archive/Redferns P52 Photo by Evening Standard/Getty Images P54-55 OLLE LINDEBORG/AFP via Getty Images P56 Photo by RB/Redferns P64 Photo by Chris Walter/WireImage P66-67, P70 Photo by Jorgen Angel/Redferns P73 Michael Putland/Getty Images P78, P91 Photo by The AGE/Fairfax Media via Getty Images via Getty Images P82, P109 Photo by Leif Skoogfors/Getty Images P84 Photo by Chris Walter/WireImage P85 Photo by Keystone/Getty Images P86L, P86R, P87, P88, P122T, P122B Photo by Gus Stewart/Redferns P90 Photo by Bob King/Redferns P99 Photo by LMPC via Getty Images P102-103 Photo by Wolfgang Kunz/ullstein bild via Getty Images P107B Photo by David Redfern/Redferns P108 Photo by Sophia MORIZET/Gamma-Rapho via Getty Images P112 Photo by Michel GINFRAY/Gamma-Rapho via Getty Images P116, P117 Photo by Gai Terrell/Redferns P137 Photo by Independent News and Media/Getty Images P166 Photo by Ake Skoglund/BIPs/Getty Images P185 Photo by Calle Hesslefors/ullstein bild via Getty Images P190 Photo by John Stoddart/Popperfoto via Getty Images P193 Photo by Ian Dickson/Redferns P208 Photo by Jon Furniss/WireImage P219, P234 JONATHAN NACKSTRAND/AFP via Getty Images P232-233 Photo by Suzan Moore for ABBA via Getty Images P238-239 Photo by Steve Wood/Daily Express/Hulton Archive/Getty Images JÖNKÖPINGS LÄNS MUSEUM: P14, P29 © Jönköpings läns museum, All Rights Reserved. AB Conny Rich Foto POLAR MUSIC P230-231 Ballie Walsh (design) REX SHUTTERSTOCK: P2, P83, P96, P98, P120, P121, P123, P124-125, P132, P155, P164B P199, P225, P228 IBL/Shutterstock P50, P153, P213 Shutterstock P71 Graham Wiltshire/Shutterstock P80 D Thorpe/Evening News/Shutterstock P89, P100 Andre Csillag/Shutterstock P101, P210 Richard Young/Shutterstock P106 George Brich/AP/Shutterstock P114 Ron Frehm/AP/Shutterstock P126-127 Katsumi Kasahara/AP/Shutterstock P160, P174 Peter Mazel/Sunshine/Shutterstock P182 Sten Rosenlund/Shutterstock P188 David Parker/ANL/Shutterstock P194 Elise Lockwood/Polygram/Australian Film Finance/Kobal/Shutterstock P206 Universal Pictures/Relativity Media/Littlestar/Playtone/Kobal/Shutterstock P211TR, P211B Universal/Kobal/Shutterstock P214L Mark Chilvers/Shutterstock P215 Eckehard Schulz/AP/Shutterstock P220 Fredrik Persson/EPA-EFE/Shutterstock ROCKSHOT: P6 Bengt H. Malmqvist © Premium Rockshot P17 Lars Åke Palén © Premium Rockshot P23 Ulf H. Holmstedt © Premium Rockshot P40 Lars Falck © Premium Rockshot P118-119, P136, P140, P141, P154, P162, P169, P170-171, P181 Anders Hanser © Premium Rockshot THE CONTENT PEOPLE: P105 Magic Moments of Rock & Pop / The Content People